Linkerd: Up and Running
A Guide to Operationalizing
a Kubernetes-Native Service Mesh

Jason Morgan and Flynn

Beijing · Boston · Farnham · Sebastopol · Tokyo

Linkerd: Up and Running

by Jason Morgan and Flynn

Copyright © 2024 Jason Morgan and Kevin Hood. All rights reserved.

Published by O'Reilly Media, Inc., 1005 Gravenstein Highway North, Sebastopol, CA 95472.

O'Reilly books may be purchased for educational, business, or sales promotional use. Online editions are also available for most titles (*http://oreilly.com*). For more information, contact our corporate/institutional sales department: 800-998-9938 or *corporate@oreilly.com*.

Acquisitions Editor: John Devins
Development Editor: Angela Rufino
Production Editor: Gregory Hyman
Copyeditor: Penelope Perkins
Proofreader: Rachel Head

Indexer: Sue Klefstad
Interior Designer: David Futato
Cover Designer: Karen Montgomery
Illustrator: Kate Dullea

April 2024: First Edition

Revision History for the First Edition
2024-04-11:   First Release

See *http://oreilly.com/catalog/errata.csp?isbn=9781098142315* for release details.

978-1-098-14231-5

[LSI]

Table of Contents

Preface

Service meshes need a little reputational rehab.

Many cloud native practitioners seem to have in mind that meshes are frightening, complex things, things to be avoided until examined as a last resort to save a dying application. We'd love to change that: service meshes are incredible tools for making developing and operating cloud native applications dramatically easier than it would otherwise be.

And, of course, we think Linkerd is the best mesh out there at making things easy for people.

So if you've been tearing your hair out trying to understand a misbehaving application based just on its logs, or if you've spent months trying to get some other mesh running and you *just want things to work*, or if you're trying to explain to yet another developer why they really don't need to worry about coding retries and mTLS into their microservice…you're in the right place. We're glad you're here.

Who Should Read This Book

This book is meant to help anyone who thinks it's easier to get things done when creating, running, or debugging microservices applications, and is looking to Linkerd to help with that. While we think that the book will benefit people who are interested in Linkerd for its own sake, Linkerd—like computing itself—is ultimately a means, not an end. This book reflects that.

Beyond that, it doesn't matter to us whether you're an application developer, a cluster operator, a platform engineer, or whatever; there should be something in here to help you get the most out of Linkerd. Our goal is to give you everything you need to get Linkerd up and running to help you get things done.

You'll need some basic knowledge of Kubernetes, the overall concept of running things in containers, and the Unix command line to get the most out of this book.

Some familiarity with Prometheus, Helm, Jaeger, etc. will also be helpful, but isn't really critical.

Why We Wrote This Book

We've both worked in the cloud native world for years and in software for many more years before that. Across all that time, the challenge that has never gone away is education; the coolest new thing on the block isn't much good until people really, truly understand what it is and how to use it.

Service meshes really should be pretty well understood by now, but of course every month there are people who need to sort out the latest and greatest changes in the meshes, and every month there are more people migrating to what is, to them, the entirely new cloud native world. We wrote this book, and we'll keep updating it, to help all these people out.

Navigating This Book

Chapter 1, "Service Mesh 101", is an introduction to service meshes: what they do, what they can help with, and why you might want to use one. This is a must-read for folks who aren't familiar with meshes.

Chapter 2, "Intro to Linkerd", takes a deep dive into Linkerd's architecture and history. If you're familiar with Linkerd already, this may be mostly recap.

Chapter 3, "Deploying Linkerd", and Chapter 4, "Adding Workloads to the Mesh", are all about getting Linkerd running in a cluster and getting your application working with Linkerd. These two chapters cover the basic nuts and bolts of actually *using* Linkerd. Chapter 5, "Ingress and Linkerd", continues by talking about the ingress problem, how to manage it, and how Linkerd interacts with ingress controllers.

Chapter 6, "The Linkerd CLI", talks about the linkerd CLI, which you can use to control and examine a Linkerd deployment.

Chapter 7, "mTLS, Linkerd, and Certificates", dives deep into Linkerd mTLS and the way it uses X.509 certificates. Chapter 8, "Linkerd Policy: Overview and Server-Based Policy", and Chapter 9, "Linkerd Route-Based Policy", continue by exploring how Linkerd can use those mTLS identities to enforce policy in your cluster.

Chapter 10, "Observing Your Platform with Linkerd", is all about Linkerd's application-wide observability mechanisms. Chapter 11, "Ensuring Reliability with Linkerd", in turn, covers how to use Linkerd to improve reliability within your application, and Chapter 12, "Multicluster Communication with Linkerd", talks about extending a Linkerd mesh across multiple Kubernetes clusters.

Chapter 13, "Linkerd CNI Versus Init Containers", addresses the thorny topic of how, exactly, you'll have Linkerd interact with the low-level networking configuration of your cluster. Unfortunately, this may be a necessary topic of discussion as you consider taking Linkerd to production, which is the topic of Chapter 14, "Production-Ready Linkerd".

Finally, Chapter 15, "Debugging Linkerd", discusses how to troubleshoot Linkerd itself, should you find things misbehaving (even though we hope you won't!).

Conventions Used in This Book

The following typographical conventions are used in this book:

Italic

Indicates new terms, URLs, email addresses, filenames, and file extensions.

`Constant width`

Used for program listings, as well as within paragraphs to refer to program elements such as variable or function names, databases, data types, environment variables, statements, and keywords.

`Constant width italic`

Shows text that should be replaced with user-supplied values or by values determined by context.

This element signifies a general note.

This element indicates a warning or caution.

Using Code Examples

Supplemental material (code examples, exercises, etc.) is available for download at *https://oreil.ly/linkerd-code*.

If you have a technical question or a problem using the code examples, please send email to *support@oreilly.com*.

This book is here to help you get your job done. In general, if example code is offered with this book, you may use it in your programs and documentation. You do not need to contact us for permission unless you're reproducing a significant portion of the code. For example, writing a program that uses several chunks of code from this book does not require permission. Selling or distributing examples from O'Reilly books does require permission. Answering a question by citing this book and quoting example code does not require permission. Incorporating a significant amount of example code from this book into your product's documentation does require permission.

We appreciate, but generally do not require, attribution. An attribution usually includes the title, author, publisher, and ISBN. For example: "*Linkerd: Up and Running* by Jason Morgan and Flynn (O'Reilly). Copyright 2024 Jason Morgan and Kevin Hood, 978-1-098-14231-5."

If you feel your use of code examples falls outside fair use or the permission given above, feel free to contact us at *permissions@oreilly.com*.

O'Reilly Online Learning

 For more than 40 years, *O'Reilly Media* has provided technology and business training, knowledge, and insight to help companies succeed.

Our unique network of experts and innovators share their knowledge and expertise through books, articles, and our online learning platform. O'Reilly's online learning platform gives you on-demand access to live training courses, in-depth learning paths, interactive coding environments, and a vast collection of text and video from O'Reilly and 200+ other publishers. For more information, visit *https://oreilly.com*.

How to Contact Us

Please address comments and questions concerning this book to the publisher:

O'Reilly Media, Inc.
1005 Gravenstein Highway North
Sebastopol, CA 95472
800-889-8969 (in the United States or Canada)
707-827-7019 (international or local)
707-829-0104 (fax)
support@oreilly.com
https://www.oreilly.com/about/contact.html

We have a web page for this book, where we list errata, examples, and any additional information. You can access this page at *https://oreil.ly/linkerd-up-and-running*.

For news and information about our books and courses, visit *https://oreilly.com*.

Find us on LinkedIn: *https://linkedin.com/company/oreilly-media*

Watch us on YouTube: *https://youtube.com/oreillymedia*

Acknowledgments

Many, many thanks to the fine folks who helped us develop this book, including (but not limited to!):

- Our editor, Angela Rufino
- Technical reviewers Daniel Bryant, Ben Muschko, and Swapnil Shevate, who provided amazing feedback that made the book worlds better
- The unsung heroes at O'Reilly who got everything into publishable shape
- Last but very much not least, the Linkerd maintainers and the fine folks at Buoyant who created the thing that we're writing about

From Flynn, a big shout out to SC and RAH for putting up with him during the year it took to put this together. Many, many thanks.

# CHAPTER 1

Service Mesh 101

Linkerd is the first service mesh—in fact, it's the project that coined the term "service mesh." It was created in 2015 by Buoyant, Inc., as we'll discuss more in Chapter 2, and for all that time it's been focused on making it easier to produce and operate truly excellent cloud native software.

But what, exactly, is a service mesh? We can start with the definition from the CNCF Glossary (*https://oreil.ly/dgNqN*):

> In a microservices world, apps are broken down into multiple smaller services that communicate over a network. Just like your wifi network, computer networks are intrinsically unreliable, hackable, and often slow. Service meshes address this new set of challenges by managing traffic (i.e., communication) between services and adding reliability, observability, and security features uniformly across all services.

The cloud native world is all about computing at a huge range of scales, from tiny clusters running on your laptop for development up through the kind of massive infrastructure that Google and Amazon wrangle. This works best when applications use the microservices architecture, but the microservices architecture is inherently more fragile than a monolithic architecture.

Fundamentally, service meshes are about hiding that fragility from the application developer—and, indeed, from the application itself. They do this by taking several features that are critical when creating robust applications and moving them from the application into the infrastructure. This allows application developers to focus on what makes their applications unique, rather than having to spend all their time worrying about how to provide the critical functions that should be the same across all applications.

In this chapter, we'll take a high-level look at what service meshes do, how they work, and why they're important. In the process, we'll provide the background you need for our more detailed discussions about Linkerd in the rest of the book.

Basic Mesh Functionality

The critical functions provided by services meshes fall into three broad categories: *security*, *reliability*, and *observability*. As we examine these three categories, we'll be comparing the way they play out in a typical monolith and in a microservices application.

Of course, "monolith" can mean several different things. Figure 1-1 shows a diagram of the "typical" monolithic application that we'll be considering.

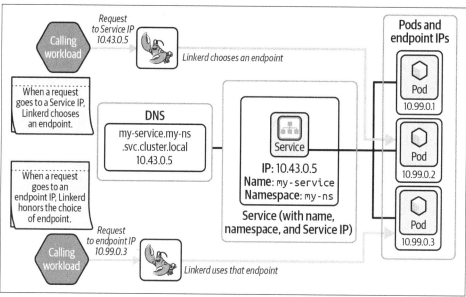

Figure 1-1. A monolithic application

The monolith is a single process within the operating system, which means that it gets to take advantage of all the protection mechanisms offered by the operating system; other processes can't see anything inside the monolith, and they *definitely* can't modify anything inside it. Communications between different parts of the monolith are typically function calls within the monolith's single memory space, so again there's no opportunity for any other process to see or alter these communications. It's true that one area of the monolith can alter the memory in use by other parts—in fact, this is a huge source of bugs!—but these are generally just errors, rather than attacks.

Multiple Processes Versus Multiple Machines

"But wait!" we hear you cry. "Any operating system worthy of the name can provide protections that do span more than one process! What about memory-mapped files or System V shared memory segments? What about the loopback interface and Unix domain sockets (to stretch the point a bit)?"

You're right: these mechanisms can allow multiple processes to cooperate and share information while still being protected by the operating system. However, they must be explicitly coded into the application, and they only function on a *single machine*. Part of the power of cloud native orchestration systems like Kubernetes is that they're allowed to schedule Pods on any machine in your cluster, and you won't know which machine ahead of time. This is tremendously flexible, but it also means that mechanisms that assume everything is on a single machine simply won't work in the cloud native world.

In contrast, Figure 1-2 shows the corresponding microservices application.

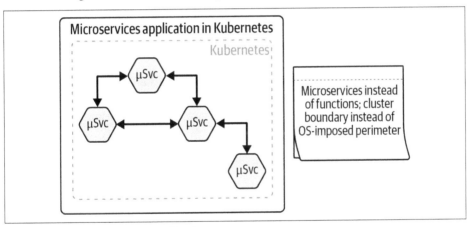

Figure 1-2. A microservices application

With microservices, things are different. Each microservice is a separate process, and microservices communicate only over the network—but the protection mechanisms provided by the operating system function only *inside* a process. These mechanisms aren't enough in a world where any information shared between microservices has to travel over the network.

This reliance on communications over the unreliable, insecure network raises a *lot* of concerns when developing microservices applications.

Security

Let's start with the fact that the network is inherently insecure. This gives rise to a number of possible issues, some of which are shown in Figure 1-3.

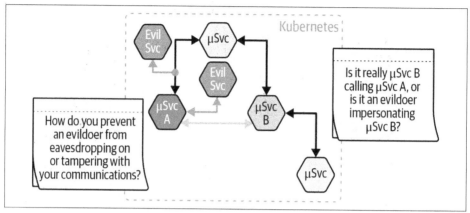

Figure 1-3. Communication is a risky business

Some of the most significant security issues are *eavesdropping, tampering, identity theft,* and *overreach:*

Eavesdropping

Evildoers may be able to intercept communications between two microservices, reading communications not intended for them. Depending on what exactly an evildoer learns, this could be a minor annoyance or a major disaster.

The typical protection against eavesdropping is *encryption*, which scrambles the data so that only the intended recipient can understand it.

Tampering

An evildoer might also be able to modify the data in transit over the network. At its simplest, the tampering attack would simply corrupt the data in transit; at its most subtle, it would modify the data to be advantageous to the attacker.

It's *extremely* important to understand that encryption alone will *not* protect against tampering! The proper protection is to use *integrity checks* like checksums; all well-designed cryptosystems include integrity checks as part of their protocols.

Identity theft

When you hand off credit card details to your payment microservice, how do you know for certain that you're really talking to your payment microservice? If an evildoer can successfully pretend to be one of your microservices, that opens the door to all manner of troublesome possibilities.

Strong *authentication* is critical to protect against this type of attack. It's the only way to be sure that the microservice you're talking to is really the one you think it is.

Overreach

On the flip side of identity theft, an evildoer may be able to take advantage of a place where a microservice is allowed to do things that it simply shouldn't be allowed to do. Imagine, for example, an evildoer finding that the payment microservice is perfectly happy to accept requests from the microservice that should merely be listing things for sale.

Careful attention to *authorization* is the key here. In a perfect world, every microservice will be able to do exactly what it needs, and no more (the *principle of least privilege*).

Reliability

Reliability in the monolith world typically refers to how well the monolith functions: when the different parts of the monolith communicate with function calls, you don't typically have to worry about a call getting lost or about one of your functions suddenly becoming unresponsive! But, as shown in Figure 1-4, unreliable communications are actually *the norm* with microservices.

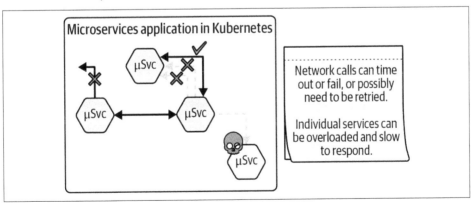

Figure 1-4. Unreliable communications are the norm

There are quite a few ways microservices can be unreliable, including:

Request failure

Sometimes requests made over the network fail. There may be any number of possible reasons, ranging from a crashed microservice to a network overload or partition. Either the application or the infrastructure needs to do something to deal with the request that failed.

In the simplest case, the mesh can simply manage *retries* for the application: if the call fails because the called service dies or times out, just resend the request. This won't always work, of course: not all requests are safe to retry, and not every failure is transient. But in many cases, simple retry logic can be used to great effect.

Service failure

A special case of request failures comes up when it isn't just a single instance of a microservice that crashes, but *all* instances. Maybe a bad version was deployed, or maybe an entire cluster crashed. In these cases the mesh can help by *failing over* to a backup cluster or to a known-good implementation of the service.

Again, this can't always happen without application help (failover of stateful services can be quite complex, for example). But microservices are often designed to manage without state, in which case mesh failover can be a huge help.

Service overload

Another special case: sometimes the failure happens because too many requests are piling onto the same service. In these cases, *circuit breaking* can help avoid a cascade failure: if the mesh fails some requests quickly, before dependent services get involved and cause further trouble, it can help limit the damage. This is a bit of a drastic technique, but this type of enforced load shedding can dramatically increase the overall reliability of the application as a whole.

Observability

It's difficult to see what's going on in any computing application: even a slow machine, these days, operates on time scales a billion times faster than the one we humans live by! Within a monolith, observability is often handled by internal logging or dashboards that collect global metrics from many different areas of the monolith. This is much less feasible with a microservices architecture, as we see in Figure 1-5— and even if it were feasible, it wouldn't tell the whole story.

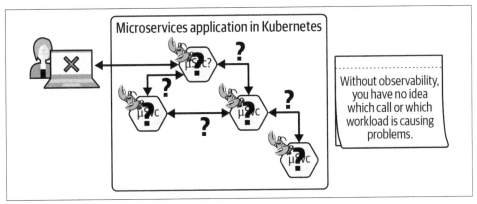

Figure 1-5. It's hard to work in the dark

In the microservices world, "observability" tends to focus more on the *call graph* and the *golden metrics*:

The call graph

When looking at a microservices application, the first critical thing is usually knowing which services are getting called by which other services. This is the *call graph*, shown in Figure 1-6, and a critical thing that a service mesh can do is to provide metrics about how much traffic is going over each edge of the graph, how much is succeeding, how much is failing, etc.

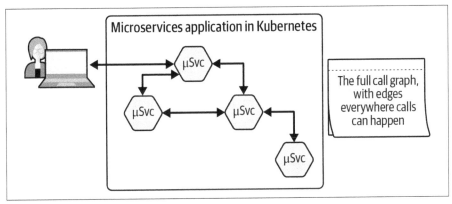

Figure 1-6. The call graph of an application

The call graph is a critical starting point because problems that the user sees from outside the cluster may actually be caused by problems with a single service buried deep in the graph. It's very important to have visibility into the whole graph to be able to solve problems.

It's also worth noting that, in specific situations, particular paths through the graph will be relevant, as shown in Figure 1-7. For example, different requests from the user may use different paths in the graph, exercising different aspects of the workloads.

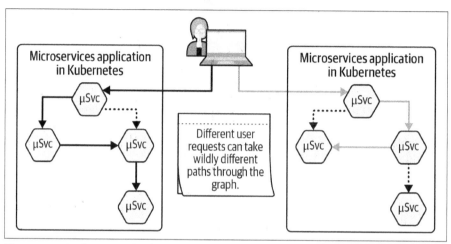

Figure 1-7. Different paths through the call graph

The golden metrics

There are a great many metrics that we could collect for every microservice. Over time, three of them have repeatedly proven especially useful in a wide variety of situations, so much so that we now refer to them as the "golden metrics" (as shown in Figure 1-8):

Latency

How long are requests taking to complete? This is typically reported as an amount of time for a certain percentage of requests to complete. For example, P95 latency indicates the time in which 95% of requests complete, so you can interpret "5 ms P95" to mean that 95% of requests complete in 5 ms or less.

Traffic

How many requests is a given service handling? This is typically reported as requests per second, or RPS.

Success rate

How many requests are succeeding? (This can also be reported as its inverse, the *error rate*.) This is typically reported as a percentage of total requests, with "success rate" often abbreviated as SR.

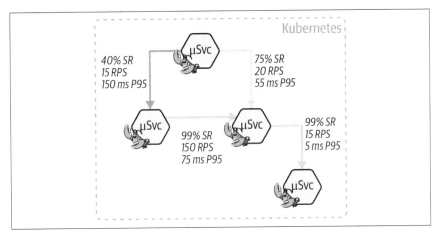

Figure 1-8. The three golden metrics

The Original "Golden Signals"

These were originally described in Google's "Monitoring Distributed Systems" post (*https://oreil.ly/TGgBm*) as the four "golden signals": latency, request rate, error rate, and saturation. We prefer "golden metrics" because metrics are things you can directly measure; you derive *signals* (like "saturation") from *metrics*.

We'll discuss these in much greater detail in Chapter 10, but it's worth noting at this point that these metrics have proven so useful that many meshes devote considerable effort to recording them—and that the service mesh is an ideal place to track them.

How Do Meshes Actually Work?

Finally, let's take a quick look at how service meshes actually function.

At a high level, all meshes are fundamentally doing the same job: they insert themselves into the operating system's network stack, take over the low-level networking that the application is using, and mediate everything the application does on the network. This is the only practical way to allow the mesh to provide all the functionality it's designed to provide without requiring changes to the application itself.

Most meshes—including Linkerd—use the *sidecar* model of injecting a proxy container next to every application container (see Figure 1-9).[1] Once running, the proxy reconfigures the host's network routing rules so that all traffic into and out of the application container goes through the proxy. This allows the proxy to control everything necessary for the functionality of the mesh.

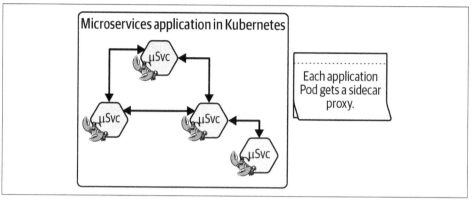

Figure 1-9. Linkerd and the sidecar model

There are other models, but the sidecar model has tremendous advantages in terms of operational simplicity and security:

- From the perspective of basically everything else in the system, the sidecar acts like it *is* part of the application. In particular, this means that all the things that the operating system does to guarantee the safety of the application just work for the sidecar, too. This is a very, very important characteristic: limiting the sidecar to exactly one security context sharply limits the attack surface of the sidecar and makes it much easier to reason about whether the things the sidecar is doing are safe.

- In much the same way, managing the sidecar is exactly the same as managing any other application or service. For example, `kubectl rollout restart` will just work to restart an application Pod *and its sidecar* as a unit.

There are disadvantages too, of course. The biggest is that *every* application Pod needs a sidecar container—even if your application has thousands of Pods. Another common concern is around latency: the sidecar, by definition, requires some time to process network traffic. Again, we'll talk more about this later, but it's worth noting up front that Linkerd goes to a lot of trouble to minimize the sidecar's impact, and in practice Linkerd is very fast and very lightweight.

---

1 The name comes from the analogy of bolting a sidecar onto a motorcycle.

So Why Do We Need This?

Put bluntly, *the functionality provided by the mesh is not optional*. You're never going to hear the engineering team say "oh, we don't need security" or "oh, reliability isn't important" (though you might have to convince people of the need for observability—hopefully this book will help!).

In other words, the choice isn't between having these three features or not: it's between having them provided by the mesh or needing to provide them in the application.

Providing them in the application is costly. Your developers could write them by hand, but this means a lot of fiddly application code replicated in every microservice, which is very easy to get wrong (especially since the temptation will always be to have senior developers focus on the crown jewels of logic specific to your business, rather than the dreary, less visible, but equally critical work of getting retries right). You may also run into incompatibilities between parts of the application, especially as the application grows.

Alternatively, you could find libraries that implement the functionality for you, which definitely saves development time. On the other hand, you still end up with each and every one of your developers needing to learn how to use those libraries, you're limited to languages and runtimes for which you can find the libraries, and incompatibilities are still a serious issue (suppose one microservice upgrades the library before another one does).

Over time, it's become pretty clear to us that pushing all this functionality into the mesh, where the application developers don't even necessarily need to know that it exists, is the smart way to provide it—and we think that Linkerd is the best of the meshes out there. If we haven't convinced you, too, by the end of the book, please reach out and let us know where we fell short!

Summary

In summary, service meshes are platform-level infrastructure that provide security, reliability, and observability uniformly across an entire application, without requiring changes to the application itself. Linkerd was the first service mesh, and we think it's still the one with the best balance of power, speed, and operational simplicity.

# CHAPTER 2

Intro to Linkerd

The year 2015 was a very good one for cloud native computing: it brought us the first Kubernetes release, the creation of the Cloud Native Computing Foundation (CNCF), and the creation of Linkerd. Linkerd was one of the first five projects donated to the CNCF, and it was the project that coined the term "service mesh."

In this chapter, you'll learn more about Linkerd, where it comes from, what makes it special, and how it works. We'll keep the history lesson short, useful, and interesting, but if you want to get right to the important information, feel free to skip ahead.

Where Does Linkerd Come From?

The Linkerd project was created in 2015 at Buoyant, Inc., by former Twitter engineers William Morgan and Oliver Gould. The first public release of Linkerd was in February 2016. You can see a brief summary of its history in Figure 2-1.

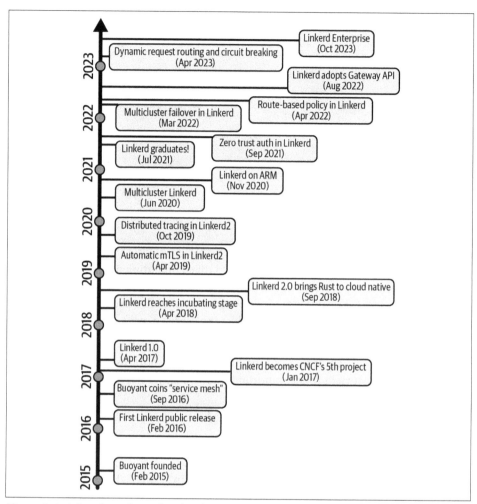

Figure 2-1. A brief timeline of Linkerd

Linkerd1

That first version of Linkerd, now called "Linkerd1," was written mostly in Scala and was largely based on the Finagle RPC library created at Twitter. It was a multiplatform mesh that supported several different container schedulers and offered a number of powerful features. However, using Finagle required Linkerd1 to run on the Java Virtual Machine (JVM), and ultimately the JVM's performance was simply too high a cost to bear.

Linkerd1 is at its end of life. Going forward, when we talk about "Linkerd," we'll be referring to modern Linkerd—Linkerd2.

Linkerd2

In 2018, the Linkerd project left the Scala world behind with a ground-up rewrite based on hard-won experience from Linkerd1 use in the real world. The project dropped support for other container orchestration engines and moved to exclusively supporting Kubernetes, with most of the code written in Go. Additionally, the developers chose to write a small, fast, purpose-built Rust proxy (creatively called `linkerd2-proxy`) to manage application communications, rather than adopting the Envoy proxy.

Linkerd and Rust

When the Linkerd2 rewrite started, the Rust programming language had been gaining attention for its memory safety, which enables developers to write code that avoids many of the memory management vulnerabilities inherent to C and C++, while still compiling to native code for high performance. The downside was that Rust's networking support was sometimes lacking features needed by Linkerd2; in many cases, the Linkerd2 developers ended up adding these features to Rust crates like `hyper` and `tokio`.

The driver behind the decisions to focus on Kubernetes and to create a purpose-built proxy was *operational simplicity*: the idea that a project should be able to deliver functionality and performance while still being simple to learn and use. This concept has had a tremendous impact on the Linkerd project as a whole, and it continues to be a major focus of Linkerd's development.

The Linkerd Proxy

It's worth repeating that `linkerd2-proxy` is *not* a general-purpose proxy; it was purpose-built for use in Linkerd. It's extremely fast and lightweight, and as a user of Linkerd, you should almost never need to interact with it directly—it is very much meant to be invisible in normal use, and most Linkerd users never need to tune or debug `linkerd2-proxy`. (In fact, the maintainers of Linkerd like to joke that the only `linkerd2-proxy` experts on the planet are…the Linkerd maintainers.)

The Linkerd control plane, introduced in the next section, will be your main interface when working with Linkerd.

Linkerd Architecture

Because Linkerd is written to be Kubernetes-native, all of its control surface is exposed in Kubernetes objects. You will manage, configure, and troubleshoot Linkerd via the Kubernetes API.

Like other service meshes, Linkerd is broken into two main components: the *data plane*, which is the part of the mesh that handles application data directly (primarily composed of the proxies), and the *control plane*, which manages the data plane. This architecture is shown in Figure 2-2.

Linkerd works by taking advantage of the Kubernetes concept of sidecars, which allows every application container to be paired with a dedicated proxy that handles all network traffic. The proxies—the data plane of the mesh—implement the advanced functionality of the mesh itself, mediating and measuring all the traffic passing through them.

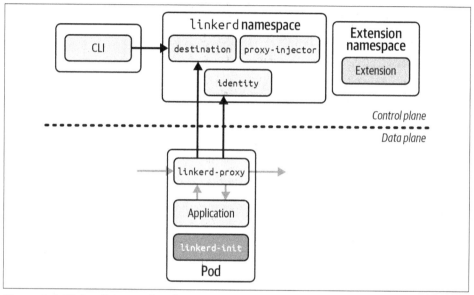

Figure 2-2. Linkerd's internal architecture

Kubernetes Sidecar Containers

Kubernetes didn't have a formal sidecar container type until the adoption of KEP-753 (*https://oreil.ly/ShohB*) in Kubernetes 1.28. The sidecar *concept* predates KEP-753 by many years, though.

Linkerd does support KEP-753 sidecar containers as of Linkerd `edge-23.11.4`, if you're running Kubernetes 1.28 or later.

Linkerd also supports the concept of *extensions*, extra microservices that run as part of the control plane to implement optional functionality (either in the cluster or in the Linkerd CLI). Some extensions (such as the Viz and Multicluster extensions) are bundled with the official Linkerd build; though they must be installed into the cluster separately, you don't need any extra tools to do so. Others (such as the SMI extension) must be obtained separately before you can install them; the documentation for the extension should tell you how to do this.

mTLS and Certificates

Linkerd relies heavily on Transport Layer Security (TLS), illustrated in Figure 2-3, for networking security—nearly all of the communications shown in Figure 2-2 are protected using TLS.

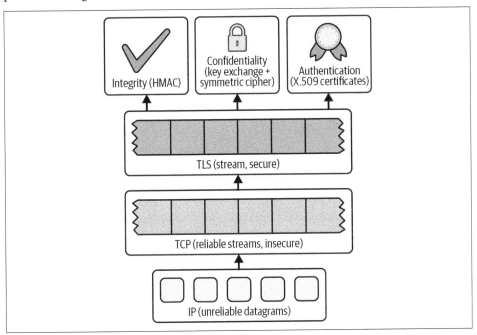

Figure 2-3. TLS architecture

TLS is the technology that's underpinned data security and privacy on the Internet for the last quarter century by allowing secure communication over an insecure network, even if the parties communicating have never done so before. It is a *huge* topic, easily worth a book on its own. We'll talk more about it in Chapter 7, but at the architectural level, it's important to understand that Linkerd uses TLS to encrypt communications within the cluster, and also as the foundation of identity within the mesh (specifically using *mutual TLS*, or *mTLS*).

In TLS, encryption and identity both rely on *keypairs*. A keypair consists of a *public key* and a *private key*, where:

- The *private* key must be known only to the single entity that the keypair identifies.

- The *public* key must be known to everyone who needs to communicate with that entity.

The keypair allows an entity (say, a workload in the Linkerd mesh) to use the private key to attest to its identity; other entities can use the public key to verify that claim.

An important note about keypairs is that they need to have a limited lifetime, so every so often we need a way to replace the keys in use for any given entity. This is called *rotating* the keys.

Certifying Authorities

Since it's very tedious to try to keep track of public and private keys separately all the time, TLS uses keys that are bundled up in *X.509 certificates* (mostly just called certificates), which give us a standard format to save the keys and a standard way to allow using one certificate to attest that another is valid. This is called *issuing* a certificate or *signing* a certificate. Organizations that support the process of issuing certificates are called *certifying authorities* or *CAs*. There are companies that treat being a CA as a core part of their business (such as Let's Encrypt, Venafi, and most cloud providers) as well as software that permits establishing CAs within our own organizations.

Using certificates to issue other certificates naturally creates a hierarchy of certificates that form a chain of trust from a single root, as shown in Figure 2-4.

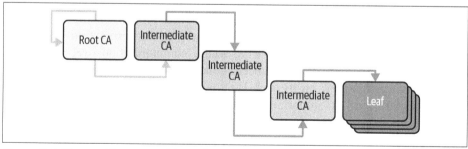

Figure 2-4. The certificate trust hierarchy

Linkerd—like everything else that uses TLS—requires a properly configured hierarchy of certificates in order to function. We'll discuss this in more detail in Chapters 3 and 7.

The Linkerd Control Plane

As of this writing, the core Linkerd control plane is composed of three primary components, as shown in Figure 2-5: the *proxy injector*, the *identity controller*, and the *destination controller*. We will discuss these components in more detail in Chapter 15. Fundamentally, they are responsible for allowing you to add individual applications to your service mesh and enabling the core security, reliability, and observability features that Linkerd provides. In order to provide these functions, these components interact directly with Linkerd's TLS certificates.

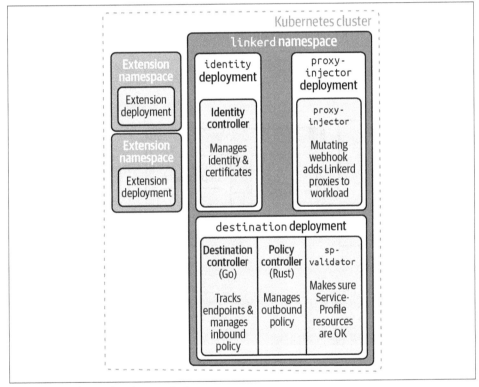

Figure 2-5. The Linkerd control plane

Linkerd Extensions

Figure 2-5 shows some extension deployments running off to the side. Linkerd extensions have no special privileges; in particular, the only way they can interact with the control plane or the proxy is via published APIs. This allows them to be written by anyone.

Several extensions are maintained by the Linkerd maintainers to supply functionality that many users want, but that isn't *required* by every Linkerd installation; these include Linkerd Viz, Linkerd Multicluster, Linkerd Jaeger, Linkerd CNI, and Linkerd SMI.

Linkerd Viz

The Linkerd Viz extension provides the Linkerd dashboard and its associated components, as shown in Figure 2-6. It also provides some additional CLI options that are useful when troubleshooting applications in your cluster.

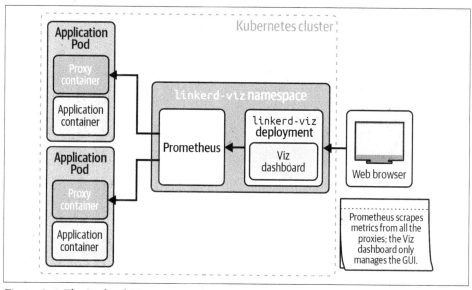

Figure 2-6. The Linkerd Viz extension

Viz is made up of the components described in the following sections.

Web. The Web component of Linkerd Viz provides the dashboard GUI used by many Linkerd operators. You don't actually need the GUI—everything it shows is accessible from the command line—but it is very commonly used, and it can be very useful.

The Linkerd Viz Dashboard Is Unauthenticated

The Linkerd Viz dashboard doesn't do user authentication—there are simply too many auth systems in use for it to be feasible. If you choose to expose Linkerd Viz to the network, you'll need to use an API gateway or the like to protect access to Linkerd Viz according to your own policies. The dashboard can't change anything in your cluster, but it does expose an awful lot of information.

You can also choose to leave the dashboard *inaccessible* from outside the cluster, and simply use the `linkerd viz dashboard` CLI command to bring up the dashboard in a web browser, via a port forward.

Tap.   Tap allows Linkerd to surface the metadata about individual requests flowing between your applications. Tap data is useful for debugging application issues in live environments, since it permits watching request and response data in real time.

Tap Doesn't Show Request Bodies

Tap can only show *metadata*: paths, headers, etc. It cannot show request *bodies*. In a great many cases, of course, the metadata is all that's needed to understand what's going on in an application.

For access to request bodies, you'll need to incorporate application-level request logging. Even in this situation, though, Tap can help narrow down the microservices and request IDs of interest when examining more detailed logs.

Tap injector.   For Linkerd Viz to surface metadata about requests, the metadata must be collected from the individual proxies in the system. The Tap injector modifies the proxy injector so that new proxies will allow this metadata collection.

Note that the proxy injector can't affect any proxy that's already running! Any workloads started before the extension was installed will need to be restarted to provide Tap data to Linkerd Viz.

Metrics API.   The metrics API is involved in collecting metrics for the Linkerd dashboard. It provides the underlying summary data for the Linkerd dashboard as well as the Linkerd CLI. Like all dashboard components, it is not involved in providing information to the Linkerd proxies.

Prometheus and Grafana.   Linkerd's Viz extension ships with a Prometheus instance. If you choose to install Grafana (as described in the Linkerd documentation (*https://oreil.ly/FB_XN*)), Linkerd publishes several open source Grafana dashboards as well.

You don't actually need Linkerd Viz to use Prometheus and Grafana. The Linkerd proxy supports Prometheus natively, so you can install Prometheus and configure it to scrape the proxies directly if you like. Linkerd Viz is simpler, though.

Always Use Your Own Prometheus

By default, installing Linkerd Viz will install an internal Prometheus instance. *Do not use this Prometheus in production*, as it does not have persistent storage configured; instead, see the Linkerd documentation (*https://oreil.ly/hI6eF*) and Example 10-9 for information about using an external Prometheus instance.

Linkerd Multicluster

The Linkerd Multicluster extension provides users the ability to connect clusters together over any public or private networks, as shown in Figure 2-7. The Multicluster extension connects clusters via a special gateway that allows all traffic to appear as if it originates locally in the cluster. This allows users to avoid configuring any special networking settings when connecting clusters. We'll dive deeper into multicluster connections in Chapter 12.

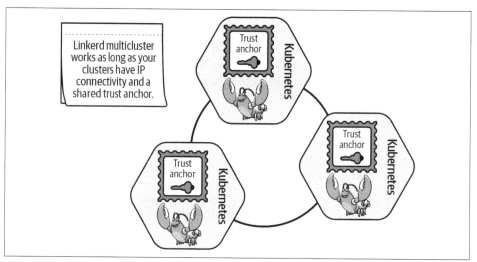

Figure 2-7. Linkerd multicluster architecture

Linkerd Jaeger

The Linkerd Jaeger extension allows Linkerd to participate in distributed tracing, as embodied by the Jaeger project (*https://oreil.ly/Dly9D*). Specifically, it allows Linkerd to emit and forward distributed tracing spans, so that you can see proxy activity in the distributed trace. As shown in Figure 2-8, Linkerd Jaeger provides a collector, which forwards spans to a Jaeger instance, and an injector, which modifies the proxy injector so that new proxies will send data to the collector. As with Linkerd Viz, you'll need to restart any workloads that were running before you installed Linkerd Jaeger!

It's important to understand that while Linkerd can aid your application-based tracing by providing details on how the proxies are contributing to your distributed application's flow, it cannot add tracing instrumentation to your application. In order to take advantage of distributed tracing with Linkerd, your application must first be configured to propagate tracing headers and create and emit its own spans.

Always Use Your Own Jaeger Instance

By default, Linkerd Jaeger will install an internal Jaeger instance. Do not use this Jaeger instance in production, as it does not provide persistent storage; instead, see the Linkerd documentation (*https://oreil.ly/QgDXC*) for information about using an external Jaeger instance.

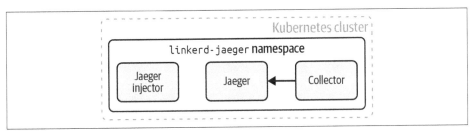

Figure 2-8. Linkerd Jaeger architecture

Linkerd CNI

When a Linkerd proxy starts running, it needs to reconfigure the kernel's network layer so that the proxy can intercept and mediate network communication for the application. There are two possible ways for Linkerd to do this: the Linkerd *init container* or the Linkerd *Container Network Interface (CNI) plugin*.

We'll discuss this in much greater detail in Chapter 13, but it's worth noting here that the CNI plugin works in conjunction with the Kubernetes CNI to reconfigure the network stack in environments where using the init container isn't possible or isn't desirable. If you do plan to use the CNI, you must install the Linkerd CNI plugin before installing any other Linkerd components. This is the only extension that can and must be installed before Linkerd's core control plane.

Linkerd SMI

The Service Mesh Interface (SMI) was a project out of the CNCF that aimed to provide a standard, cross-platform API to control the behavior of a service mesh.

The Linkerd SMI extension allows Linkerd to do traffic splitting using the SMI TrafficSplit custom resource definition (CRD).[1]

SMI saw somewhat mixed adoption overall, and as of October 2023 the SMI project was archived, with many of its concepts and goals used to inform the GAMMA initiative within Gateway API (*https://oreil.ly/J1BOK*), which Linkerd supports as of version 2.14.

Summary

Linkerd got started in 2015 and grew into its modern form, based on Rust and Go and driven by the concept of operational simplicity, in 2018. That focus on operational simplicity remains today and is borne out by Linkerd's architecture, with a small, purpose-built Rust data plane proxy, a Go control plane that focuses on critical functionality, and a set of extensions for optional functionality.

---

1 There were other SMI CRDs, but other than TrafficSplit, they duplicate functionality that Linkerd already had APIs for.

# CHAPTER 3

Deploying Linkerd

Now that you understand what Linkerd is and a bit about how it works, it's time to dig into deploying Linkerd in your environment. We're going to dive into the whats, whys, and hows of installing Linkerd in this chapter. You can also check out the official Linkerd docs to review the getting started guide (*https://oreil.ly/Pyiwx*).

Considerations

Installing Linkerd can often be quick, easy, and painless. Unfortunately, some of that ease of use can mask real pitfalls that you'll want to avoid. We'll dive more into the specifics when we get to the install section—for now, suffice it to say that when you install Linkerd in your actual non-demo environments, you'll want to be sure to plan for generating and storing the TLS certificates we briefly described in Chapter 2. You'll also want to be sure you have a good understanding of all non-HTTP ports being used by your applications, so that you can configure *protocol discovery* correctly for them (this is covered in more detail in Chapter 4).

Linkerd Versioning

We mentioned in Chapter 2 that this book is focused exclusively on Linkerd2, the second major version of Linkerd, which is effectively a rewrite of the project. In recognition of that, Linkerd uses a versioning system that looks like semantic versioning (*https://semver.org*) but is, in fact, distinct. Linkerd has two major release channels: *stable* and *edge*. You can read more about this versioning scheme and release model in the official Linkerd documentation (*https://oreil.ly/7igL_*).

Stable

The stable channel is used for vendor releases, such as Buoyant Enterprise for Linkerd (from, unsurprisingly, Buoyant). This channel uses a modified semantic versioning scheme:

```
stable-2.<major>.<minor>.<patch>
```

This means that when you see, for example, "Linkerd 2.12.3," the major version is 12 and the minor version is 3. This release has no patch number.

The rules of semantic versioning are that a change to the major version means that Linkerd has introduced breaking changes or significant new capabilities, while a change to only the minor version indicates that the new release is fully backward compatible with the previous version and includes improvements or bug fixes. Patch releases are rare and indicate a security fix has been issued for a given minor version.

Edge

The edge release channel is where you'll find releases of pure open source Linkerd, built from the latest changes to Linkerd available when they're released. Edge releases are generally provided on a weekly basis with the following versioning scheme:

```
edge-<two digit year>.<month>.<number within the month>
```

For example, `edge-24.1.1` would be the first edge release of the first month of the year 2024.

> **Edge Releases Do Not Use Semantic Versioning**
>
> It's probably obvious that the edge release channel does *not* use semantic versioning, but it's worth reiterating that point. It's extremely important that you read the release notes for any edge release you install, and that you provide feedback to the Linkerd team about your experiences.

Workloads, Pods, and Services

Linkerd is a service mesh that is designed around Kubernetes. This means that, unlike many other service mesh options, you can use Linkerd without ever interacting with any of its custom resource definitions. Linkerd uses Kubernetes constructs like workloads, Pods, and services to manage the majority of its routing and configuration options—so if you have something that runs in Kubernetes today, you can add Linkerd to it and it should behave the same, just with the benefits of Linkerd added to it. (See Figure 3-1.) There are some exceptions to this that we'll detail in Chapter 4.

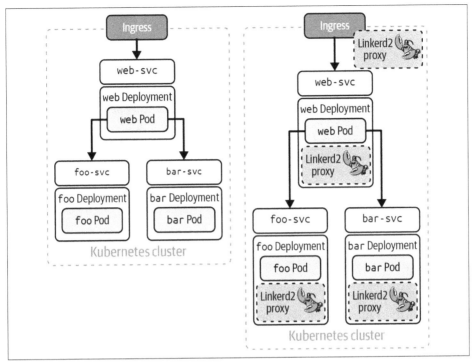

Figure 3-1. Adding Linkerd should never break your application

TLS certificates

As we mentioned in Chapter 2, Linkerd relies on TLS certificates in a particular hierarchy to provide identity within the mesh. Specifically, Linkerd requires a single *trust anchor* certificate, which signs an *identity issuer* certificate, which signs *workload certificates* (one per workload in the mesh). This is shown in Figure 3-2.

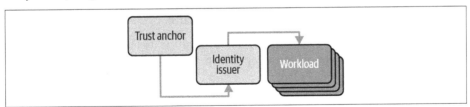

Figure 3-2. The Linkerd trust hierarchy

Linkerd manages workload certificates for you, but you'll need to work with a certifying authority to manage the trust anchor and identity issuer certificates. In this chapter, we'll describe how this works with CLI and Helm installs.

Linkerd Viz

We mentioned Linkerd Viz briefly in Chapter 2: it's Linkerd's open source dashboard component, providing an easy-to-use metrics collection and presentation system for Linkerd. It can collect useful metrics about all meshed workloads and present them in a simple web UI. The dashboard can provide the following details about your Linkerd environment:

- Detailed application metrics, broken down by:
  — Namespace
  — Workload
  — Pod
  — Service
- Information about connections between your workloads, including:
  — TLS status
  — Meshed status
  — Workload identity
  — Paths and headers in use (via Viz Tap)
  — Metrics breakdowns on a path-by-path basis

We'll discuss using Linkerd Viz in more detail in Chapter 10, and we'll discuss production concerns for Linkerd Viz in Chapter 14.

The Linkerd Viz Dashboard Is Unauthenticated

As discussed in Chapter 2, the Linkerd Viz dashboard doesn't do user authentication. It's up to you to be careful about how you make it available to users.

Linkerd Viz is considered part of the Linkerd core, but it must be installed separately since some Linkerd installations completely replace Viz with custom-built systems. In general, we strongly recommend installing Viz unless you have a strong reason not to. In the following instructions, we will include installing Viz.

Always Use Your Own Prometheus

By default, installing Linkerd Viz will install an internal Prometheus instance. *Do not use this Prometheus in production*, as it does not have persistent storage configured; instead, see the Linkerd documentation (*https://oreil.ly/hI6eF*) and Example 10-9 for information about using an external Prometheus instance.

Deploying Linkerd

To deploy Linkerd, you'll need to have a Kubernetes cluster available. This guide will use a k3s (*https://k3s.io*) cluster deployed locally using the k3d (*https://k3d.io*) tool. If you're already comfortable installing and deploying Linkerd, feel free to skip ahead to Chapter 4.

Required Tools

For the rest of this book, we're going to assume you have the following tools available:

- kubectl (*https://oreil.ly/WPcEB*)
- Helm (*https://oreil.ly/HMIQw*)
- The linkerd CLI (*https://oreil.ly/OjxD2*)
- k3d (*https://k3d.io*)
- The step CLI (*https://oreil.ly/Y40gA*)

Provisioning a Kubernetes Cluster

Start by creating a k3d cluster:

```
$ k3d cluster create linkerd
```

k3d will provision your Kubernetes cluster and update your KUBECONFIG. You can test your connection to your new cluster by running:

```
$ kubectl get nodes
```

You should also validate that the cluster is configured correctly and that you have the appropriate permissions for the install by running a preinstall check via the Linkerd CLI:

```
$ linkerd check --pre
```

Installing Linkerd via the CLI

The Linkerd CLI makes it easy to get started with a Linkerd install. It will generate the Kubernetes manifests required to install Linkerd and allow you to easily apply them to your cluster.

The linkerd install Command and Certificates

When you install Linkerd from the CLI, you have the option of specifying certificates for it to use. If you don't, it will silently create certificates for you, as shown in Figure 3-3. This makes Linkerd very easy to deploy, but it causes some operational headaches when the time comes to rotate certificates, *because linkerd install does not save the trust anchor's private key—anywhere*. We'll talk about this in more detail in Chapter 7.

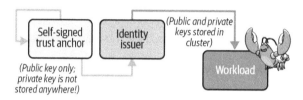

Figure 3-3. The trust hierarchy created with the linkerd install command

---

Run the following commands to install Linkerd via the CLI:

```
$ linkerd install --crds | kubectl apply -f -
```

This will install the Linkerd CRDs in your cluster. As of Linkerd 2.12, installing Linkerd's CRDs is done using a separate chart and requires its own command when running an install. Following the CRD install, you'll need to continue the installation by installing the core Linkerd control plane:

```
$ linkerd install | kubectl apply -f -
```

With this complete, the Linkerd control plane will begin setting itself up in your cluster. You'll soon have access to all the tools you need to run a minimal Linkerd service mesh. You can confirm the install has completed successfully by running:

```
$ linkerd check
```

Production Clusters Need Production Certificates

Again, if you don't explicitly say otherwise, linkerd install will silently create certificates for you. This is OK for a demo, but *not* for production.

After installing the core Linkerd control plane, you can install Linkerd Viz:

```
$ linkerd viz install | kubectl apply -f -
```

As with Linkerd itself, this will start the install and then immediately return. To wait for it to finish and confirm that installation was successful, run:

```
$ linkerd check
```

Always Use Your Own Prometheus

By default, installing Linkerd Viz will install an internal Prometheus instance. *Do not use this Prometheus in production*, as it does not have persistent storage configured; instead, see the Linkerd documentation (*https://oreil.ly/hI6eF*) and Example 10-9 for information about using an external Prometheus instance.

Installing Linkerd via Helm

The folks at Buoyant, the makers of Linkerd, recommend in their production runbook guide (*https://oreil.ly/ZjDzr*) that you use Helm to install and manage Linkerd in production. Helm provides a well tested, documented, and supported path for installing and upgrading Linkerd (and in fact, the Linkerd CLI actually uses Helm templates under the hood to generate its Kubernetes manifests).

Using the Helm-based install also requires you to think more about certificate management up front, which simplifies the process of renewing your certificates later. We'll cover certificates in (much) more detail in Chapter 7; for now, let's walk through a simple Helm installation with manually generated certificates.

Generate Linkerd certificates

The simplest way to install Linkerd with Helm is to manually generate the two certificates that every Linkerd installation requires: the trust anchor and the identity issuer. We'll use the Smallstep CLI, `step`, to do this, as illustrated in Example 3-1.

Certificates and Security

We're generating certificates here without giving any real thought to how to safely manage the private keys. This is OK for a demo, but *not* for production use. We'll get into this more in Chapter 7.

Example 3-1. Creating certificates for Linkerd

```
# Start by creating your root certificate, which Linkerd refers to
# as the trust anchor certificate.
$ step certificate create root.linkerd.cluster.local ca.crt ca.key \
  --profile root-ca --no-password --insecure
```

```
# Next, create the intermediary certificate. Linkerd refers to this
# as the identity issuer certificate.
$ step certificate create identity.linkerd.cluster.local issuer.crt issuer.key \
  --profile intermediate-ca --not-after 8760h --no-password --insecure \
  --ca ca.crt --ca-key ca.key
```

After running these commands, you'll have the trust hierarchy shown in Figure 3-4. Your laptop will be holding both the public and private keys for the trust anchor and the identity issuer, and the identity issuer's cert will be signed by the trust anchor. (There aren't any workload certs yet: Linkerd will create those when it's installed in the cluster.)

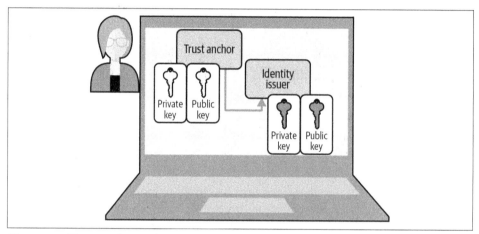

Figure 3-4. The trust hierarchy created with the `step` *command*

Keep the Keys!

Remember, in the real world, it's *very important* to keep the private key safe. Even for our more academic use here, keep it around—you'll want it when we talk about certificate rotation in Chapter 7.

The Linkerd docs cover creating certificates in some detail (*https://oreil.ly/BPO3F*). Please refer to the latest version of the docs if you run into any difficulty.

Helm install

After generating certificates, you can install Linkerd with Helm using the commands in Example 3-2. Once again, the official docs have the most up-to-date instructions; however, it's very important to understand what the `--set-file` arguments shown in Example 3-2 do:

- `--set-file identityTrustAnchorsPEM` tells Helm the file from which to copy the trust anchor's public key. This is the only key we need for the trust anchor.

- `--set-file identity.issuers.tls.crtPEM` and `--set-file identity.issuers.tls.keyPEM` tell Helm the files from which to copy the identity issuer's public and private keys, respectively. Both are required.

Example 3-2. Installing Linkerd with Helm

```
# Add the Linkerd stable repo
$ helm repo add linkerd https://helm.linkerd.io/stable

# Update your Helm repositories
$ helm repo update

# Install the Linkerd CRDs
$ helm install linkerd-crds linkerd/linkerd-crds \
  -n linkerd --create-namespace

# Install the Linkerd control plane
$ helm install linkerd-control-plane \
  -n linkerd \
  --set-file identityTrustAnchorsPEM=ca.crt \
  --set-file identity.issuer.tls.crtPEM=issuer.crt \
  --set-file identity.issuer.tls.keyPEM=issuer.key \
  linkerd/linkerd-control-plane

# Ensure your install was successful
$ linkerd check
```

The `linkerd check` command will let you know the current state of Linkerd in your cluster. It's useful for ensuring your install completed successfully.

Once `helm install` completes, the cluster will have copies of the keys Linkerd needs to run, as shown in Figure 3-5. The keys will, of course, still be present on your laptop, so be careful with them!

Permissions Matter!

Note that the trust anchor's private key is *not* present in the cluster, but the identity issuer's private key *is* present in the cluster. This is required for Linkerd to work. In the real world, you'll want to make sure that Linkerd itself is the only thing that can see that key. This is covered in more detail in Chapter 7.

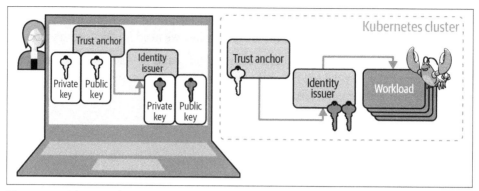

Figure 3-5. The trust hierarchy created after `helm install`

Finally, we can install Linkerd Viz using its Helm chart:

```
$ helm install linkerd-viz linkerd/linkerd-viz \
-n linkerd-viz --create-namespace
```

As before, we'll monitor the installation to make sure that it succeeds:

```
$ linkerd check
```

Always Use Your Own Prometheus

By default, installing Linkerd Viz will install an internal Prometheus instance. *Do not use this Prometheus in production*, as it does not have persistent storage configured; instead, see the Linkerd documentation (*https://oreil.ly/hI6eF*) and Example 10-9 for information about using an external Prometheus instance.

Configuring Linkerd

Now that you've completed an install of Linkerd's core control plane, we're going to pause and take a look at what options you have for configuring the Linkerd control plane in your cluster. This is necessarily going to be a summary of common configuration points for the control plane, not an exhaustive list.

As of Linkerd 2.12, the control plane is managed and configured via the `linkerd-control-plane` Helm chart. The following settings provide important configuration points for Linkerd. The particular settings can be found by reviewing the current Helm chart values using the following command:

```
$ helm show values linkerd/linkerd-control-plane
```

We'll talk about the general settings, and you'll need to map them to the appropriate locations in your values file. See Chapter 14 for some examples of Linkerd Helm values files.

Cluster Networks

Linkerd doesn't have a way to read your cluster network settings at install time, so the `linkerd-control-plane` Helm chart assumes that your cluster is using one of the common network ranges for its cluster network. If your cluster's IP addresses are not in one of the following ranges, you'll need to override the IP range at install time:

```
10.0.0.0/8, 100.64.0.0/10, 172.16.0.0/12, 192.168.0.0/16
```

Linkerd Control Plane Resources

The default install of Linkerd doesn't set resource requests or limits. You should consider setting requests and limits for your control plane components to aid in scheduling Pods and ensuring Linkerd has the resources it needs to function. Be cautious: as of Linkerd 2.12 the Linkerd destination component has a fairly fixed memory footprint that scales with the number of endpoints in your cluster. If the memory limit you set is too low, you may find yourself in a loop of destination components being "out of memory killed," or OOMKilled.

Opaque and Skip Ports

Opaque ports and skip ports are Linkerd names for ports to which special rules are applied. You'll want to review the relevant Linkerd docs (*https://oreil.ly/_H929*) for the most up-to-date information on the topic. We'll give a brief overview of the concepts here; you'll find many more details in Chapter 4.

An *opaque* port in Linkerd is a port that should be treated as a generic TCP connection. Linkerd will still use mTLS on opaque traffic, but it will *not* perform protocol detection or any kind of protocol-specific logic, so the end result will be similar to the way simple, connection-oriented network load balancing works. A port should be marked as opaque at install time if you know it will be part of the mesh and serving non-HTTP TCP traffic.

Remember, there is *no* protocol detection, and thus *no* request metrics or per-request load balancing, on opaque ports.

This section is dedicated to discussing global, install-time Linkerd configuration values. Any opaque port set at install time will be applied globally to all workloads.

Default Opaque Ports

The following ports are the defaults configured at install time:

- SMTP: 25 and 587
- MySQL: 3306 and, when used with Galera, 4444. (Ports 4567 and 4568 might also be used by Galera, but they're not opaque by default.)
- PostgreSQL: 5432
- Redis: 6379
- Elasticsearch: 9300
- Memcached: 11211

By contrast, a *skip* port is one that you instruct Linkerd to completely ignore. Skipped traffic will completely bypass the proxy; the mesh will not handle it at all. Notably, *Linkerd cannot encrypt traffic over skip ports.*

Unlike opaque ports, you need to tell Linkerd whether skip ports refer to inbound traffic, outbound traffic, or both.

Default Skip Ports

Ports 4567 and 4568 (Galera) are ignored by default in a standard Linkerd install.

Summary

You should now have a good sense of how to install Linkerd as well as an understanding of the major configuration points in Linkerd. You should also have a good grasp of the potential points of friction with installing Linkerd: specifically, generating certificates and handling non-HTTP traffic. While you can use either the Linkerd CLI or the Linkerd Helm charts to install Linkerd, we recommend that you default to using Helm.

# CHAPTER 4

Adding Workloads to the Mesh

Getting Linkerd running in your cluster is a great first step. But it's pointless to run Linkerd with nothing else: to get actual value out of your Linkerd cluster, you'll need to get workloads running in your service mesh. In this chapter, we'll show you how to do exactly that.

Workloads Versus Services

We'll talk about "workloads" a lot in this chapter—but sometimes we'll also talk about "services," and sometimes "Services." Unfortunately, these three things all have slightly different meanings:

Service
> A Kubernetes resource that is widely used to control how Kubernetes allocates DNS names and IP addresses for services (see Figure 4-1).

Workload
> A thing that actually does work on your behalf. A workload receives requests over the network and executes code to take actions. In Kubernetes, it's usually one or more Pods (to provide the computation), often managed by a Deployment or DaemonSet resource, plus one or more Services (to manage the names and IP addresses), as illustrated in Figure 4-1.

service
> A less formal term that could refer to either a Service or a workload, depending on context. This lack of precision shows just one of many cases where Kubernetes terminology is very much more confusing than we would like it to be.

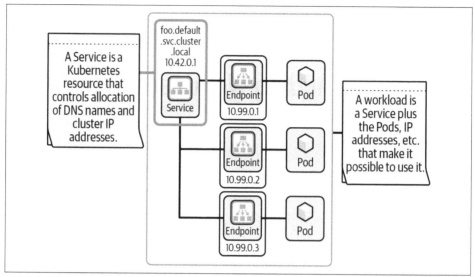

Figure 4-1. The workload as distinct from the Service

As an application developer, you can usually just say "service" and trust that people will be fine with the ambiguity. Unfortunately, we often need to be more precise when talking about service meshes—hence the discussion of *workloads* here rather than *services*.

What Does It Mean to Add a Workload to the Mesh?

"Adding a workload to the mesh" really means "adding the Linkerd sidecar to each of your workload's Pods," as shown in Figure 4-2.

Ultimately, this means changing the Pod's definition to include the sidecar container. While you *could* do this by manually editing the YAML that defines the Pod, it's much easier and safer to let Linkerd do the heavy lifting instead.

Linkerd includes a Kubernetes admission controller called the `linkerd-proxy-injector`. Its job, unsurprisingly, is to inject Linkerd proxies into workload Pods. Of course, it doesn't do this blindly; instead, it looks for Kubernetes annotations that tell it which Pods need to be injected, as shown in Figure 4-3.

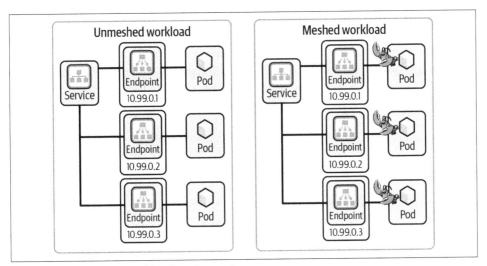

Figure 4-2. Adding a workload to the mesh

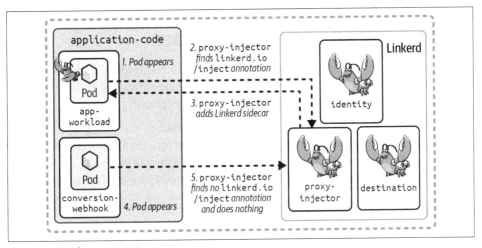

Figure 4-3. The proxy injector

Injecting Individual Workloads

The most common way to handle injection is to add the `linkerd.io/inject: enabled` annotation directly to the Pod itself, typically by adding the annotation to the Pod template in a Deployment, DaemonSet, etc. Whenever `linkerd-proxy-injector` sees a new Pod with this annotation, it will inject the proxy sidecar into the Pod for you.

It's worth pointing out that the value of the annotation is important: `enabled` means to do a normal sidecar injection. We'll look at other values shortly.

All Pods Are Created Equal

It doesn't matter what kind of resource is being used to create the Pod. Deployments, DaemonSets, hand-tooled ReplicaSets, Argo Rollouts resources—all of them create their Pods exactly the same way. What the Linkerd injector notices is that a new Pod exists, not what caused it to be created.

Injecting All Workloads in a Namespace

You can add the `linkerd.io/inject` annotation to a Namespace, rather than to a Pod. Once that's done, every new Pod created in that namespace will be injected (and, again, it *does not matter* what causes the new Pod to be created).

This can be very useful for situations where automation is creating Pods, but it's difficult or error-prone to modify the annotations on the Pods themselves. For example, some ingress controllers will re-create Deployments every time you change a resource; rather than mess about with laboriously modifying the Pod template used by the ingress controller (if it's even possible), you can just annotate the Namespace in which the Deployments will be created.

linkerd.io/inject Values

The value of the `linkerd.io/inject` annotation does matter—it's not just a matter of having a non-empty string there. There are three specific values that are meaningful:

`linkerd.io/inject: enabled`
   The most common case: `linkerd-proxy-injector` will add a proxy container to the Pod and tell the proxy to run in its "normal" mode.

```
linkerd.io/inject: ingress
```
linkerd-proxy-injector will add a proxy container to the Pod, but the proxy will run in "ingress" mode (which we'll discuss in Chapter 5).

```
linkerd.io/inject: disabled
```
This explicitly tells linkerd-proxy-injector to *not* add the proxy sidecar, even if there's a Namespace annotation that would otherwise say to add the sidecar.

We'll discuss ingress mode more in Chapter 5: it's a workaround for ingress controllers that only know how to route requests directly to workload endpoints. In most cases, you should use linkerd.io/inject: enabled to get "normal" mode.

Why Might You Decide Not to Add a Workload to the Mesh?

In general:

- You always want to add your application workloads to the mesh.
- You never want to add cluster infrastructure to the mesh.

So, for example, things in the kube-system namespace are never injected. All of these Pods are designed to protect themselves no matter what else is going on, and some of them need to be sure that nothing is between them and the network layer, so you shouldn't inject them.

Likewise, a Kubernetes conversion webhook (as shown in the application-code namespace in Figure 4-3) generally shouldn't be in the mesh. The webhook mechanism itself already makes specific demands around TLS, and the mesh won't help with that. (It probably won't hurt, but there's really no point.) Another good example here is CNI implementations: these need direct access to the network layer and shouldn't be injected.

On the other hand, the workloads that are part of your application running in the cluster should always be injected into the mesh. All of these guidelines are shown in Figure 4-4.

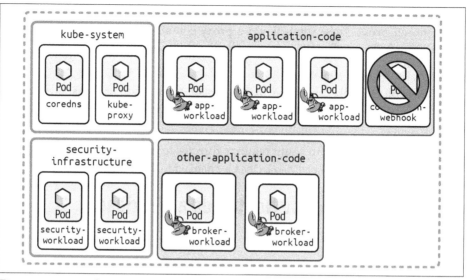

Figure 4-4. Inject the application, not the infrastructure

Other Proxy Configuration Options

Although the basic `linkerd.io/inject` annotation is the only proxy configuration option you *must* provide, there are actually quite a few other things you can configure about the proxy. The full list can be found in the Linkerd Proxy Configuration documentation (*https://oreil.ly/9FiJF*), but two areas very much worth learning about from the start are *protocol detection* and *Kubernetes resource limits*.

Protocol Detection

As we discussed in Chapter 1, Linkerd puts a lot of effort into operational simplicity; whenever possible, Linkerd tries to make sure things just work when you bring your application into the mesh. Protocol detection is a critical part of this, because Linkerd has to know the protocol being used over a connection to correctly manage the connection, as shown in Figure 4-5.

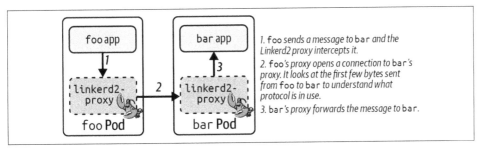

Figure 4-5. Protocol detection

There are several reasons that Linkerd (or any other mesh) needs to know the protocol in use over the wire. We'll touch on just a few of them:

Observability

Linkerd can't provide proper metrics without understanding the flow of the protocol. Identifying the beginning and end of a request is crucial to measuring request rate and latency. Reading the status of a request is critical to measuring the success rate.

Reliability

Any reliability feature beyond the most basic requires understanding the protocol in flight. Consider load balancing, for example: if Linkerd doesn't know the protocol, it can only do connection-based load balancing, where an incoming TCP connection is assigned to a specific workload Pod.

However, connection-based load balancing doesn't work very well for protocols like HTTP/2 and gRPC. In these protocols, a single long-lived connection can carry many requests, with multiple requests active at the same time. Linkerd can dramatically improve reliability and performance by assigning individual requests to workload Pods, rather than fixing an entire connection to a Pod. (It's a fun Linkerd fact that it does this automatically, with zero configuration; just install Linkerd, and you get this for free.)

Security

If a workload makes a TLS connection to another workload, Linkerd shouldn't try to reencrypt it. It also shouldn't try to do anything fancy with load balancing, since it won't be able to see anything inside the connection. (This implies that you'll get the best results with Linkerd by having your workloads *not* use TLS when connecting to each other: let Linkerd do mTLS for you!)

When Protocol Detection Goes Wrong

Automatic protocol detection has one major limitation: it can only work for protocols where the entity that makes the connection is also the first one to send data (*client-speaks-first* protocols). It will fail for protocols where the entity that *receives* the connection is the first to send data (*server-speaks-first* protocols).

The reason for this limitation is that until Linkerd knows the protocol, it can't make reasonable decisions about how to do load balancing, so it can't decide what server to connect to, so it can't find out what the server will say! Every proxy has this frustratingly circular issue.

In the cloud native world, many—perhaps most?—common protocols are, happily, client-speaks-first protocols; for example, HTTP, gRPC, and TLS itself are all client-speaks-first. Unfortunately, there are some important server-speaks-first protocols out there: SMTP, MySQL, and Redis are all examples.

If Linkerd cannot detect the protocol, it will assume it's a raw TCP connection, simply because that's the least common denominator that will always function. The problem is that for server-speaks-first protocols, Linkerd will wait 10 seconds before assuming that it won't be able to detect the protocol, and that 10-second delay is obviously not what you want. To prevent that, you need to tell Linkerd that it should either skip the connection entirely or treat it as opaque.

Opaque Ports Versus Skip Ports

When you tell Linkerd to *skip* a connection, you're telling it to have absolutely nothing to do with that connection. In fact, the Linkerd proxies don't touch the connection at all: the packets flow straight from workload to workload.

This means that Linkerd can't do mTLS, load balancing, metrics collection, or *anything*. The connection effectively happens outside the mesh entirely.

An *opaque* connection, on the other hand, does pass through the Linkerd proxies, which means that it is carried over mTLS. It's still encrypted and Linkerd still enforces any policy that has been configured, but you'll only get per-connection metrics and load balancing (because Linkerd knows that it can't see into the stream to look at individual requests).

This distinction is shown in Figure 4-6.

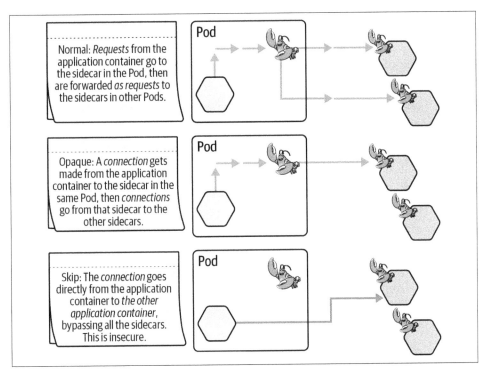

Figure 4-6. Opaque ports versus skip ports

This all implies that if you need to use server-speaks-first protocols, it's better to mark them as opaque, rather than skipping them entirely. Skipping should only be necessary when the destination of the traffic isn't part of your mesh. Since opaque connections still rely on a Linkerd proxy to do mTLS, they can't work if there's no proxy there to receive the connection!

Configuring Protocol Detection

There are two ways to tell Linkerd about protocols. You can use a Server resource, which we'll cover when we talk policy in Chapter 8, or you can use the following annotations to mark specific ports as opaque or skipped:

`config.linkerd.io/opaque-ports`
    Connections to or from these ports will always be treated as opaque.

`config.linkerd.io/skip-inbound-ports`
    Connections coming into this workload on these ports will always be skipped.

`config.linkerd.io/skip-outbound-ports`
    Connections leaving this workload on these ports will always be skipped.

All of these take comma-separated lists of port numbers or port ranges, so all of the following are legal:

`config.linkerd.io/opaque-ports: 25`
> This will treat only port 25 as opaque.

`config.linkerd.io/skip-inbound-ports: 3300,9900`
> This will skip connections coming in on port 3300 or 9900.

`config.linkerd.io/skip-inbound-ports: 8000-9000`
> This will skip connections coming in on any port between 8000 and 9000, inclusive.

`config.linkerd.io/skip-outbound-ports: 25,587,8000-9000`
> This will skip connections going out on port 25, port 587, or any port between 8000 and 9000, inclusive.

There's also a `config.linkerd.io/skip-subnets` option, which skips any connection to or from any listed subnets. Its argument is a comma-separated list of Classless Inter-Domain Routing (CIDR) (*https://oreil.ly/soiAU*) ranges—for example, `config.linkerd.io/skip-subnets: 10.0.0.0/8,192.168.1.0/24`.

Default Opaque Ports

As of Linkerd 2.12, several ports are marked as opaque by default (see the list in "Default Opaque Ports" on page 36 for details).

The default ports are meant to allow various server-speaks-first protocols, such as MySQL and SMTP, to work seamlessly with Linkerd. If you're using these ports for client-speaks-first protocols, you'll need to use a Server resource to override the port default (or—better—just choose a different port for your client-speaks-first protocol!).

Kubernetes Resource Limits

Compared to protocol detection, Kubernetes resource limits are much more straightforward. There's a simple set of annotations to set that will allow you to specify resource requests and limits, as shown in Table 4-1.

Table 4-1. Linkerd annotations for resource requests and limits

Annotation	Effect
`config.linkerd.io/proxy-cpu-limit`	Maximum amount of CPU units that the proxy sidecar can use
`config.linkerd.io/proxy-cpu-request`	Amount of CPU units that the proxy sidecar requests
`config.linkerd.io/proxy-ephemeral-storage-limit`	Used to override the `limitEphemeralStorage` config
`config.linkerd.io/proxy-ephemeral-storage-request`	Used to override the `requestEphemeralStorage` config
`config.linkerd.io/proxy-memory-limit`	Maximum amount of memory that the proxy sidecar can use
`config.linkerd.io/proxy-memory-request`	Amount of memory that the proxy sidecar requests

Summary

So there you have it: the start-to-finish guide for getting your workloads to be an effective part of the Linkerd mesh. Hopefully you now have a good understanding of how to make everything work, and of the gotchas along the way (like server-speaks-first protocols). Next up is getting Linkerd and ingress controllers to play nicely together.

# CHAPTER 5

Ingress and Linkerd

Whenever you work with Kubernetes, you always have to find a way for your users *outside* your cluster to be able to make requests of (some of) the services running *inside* your cluster. This is the *ingress problem* (see Figure 5-1): the cluster wants to protect everything inside from the big scary Internet, but that's where your legitimate users are.

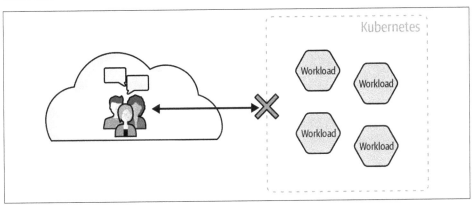

Figure 5-1. The ingress problem

There's an entire class of applications out there, unsurprisingly called *ingress controllers*, whose sole purpose is solving the ingress problem. Linkerd does not include an ingress controller; instead, it allows you to mesh whatever ingress controller you like, as long as certain rules are followed. In this chapter, you'll learn how to make Linkerd and the ingress controller of your choice play nicely with each other.

There are a lot of different ingress controllers, which approach the ingress problem in fascinatingly different ways. However, there are some common threads across all of them, shown in Figure 5-2.

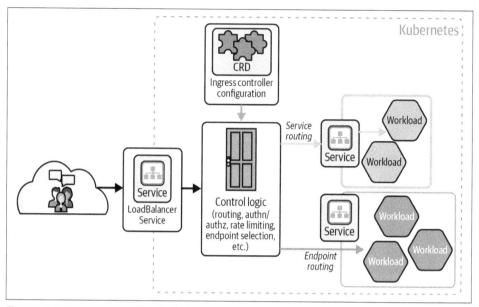

Figure 5-2. Ingress controller high-level architecture

These common threads include:

- They are all designed to live right at the edge of a cluster (usually behind a Kubernetes Service of type `LoadBalancer`), exposed directly to the Internet so that their clients can reach them. Security is always a major concern for an ingress controller.

- They always have a way to control which requests from outside get routed to which services inside. This is another critical security issue: installing an ingress controller cannot mean that all the services in your cluster are open to the Internet.

All the popular ingress controllers support sophisticated routing controls at OSI layer 7 (*https://oreil.ly/S-sjB*), typically focusing on HTTP and gRPC. Many also support more limited control for routing OSI layer 4 connections:

- At OSI layer 7 (the application layer), the ingress controller might have capabilities like "route an HTTP request where the hostname is `foo.example.com` and the `path` starts with `/bar/` to the Service named `bar-service`."

- At OSI layer 4 (the transport layer), its capabilities are more likely to be along the lines of "route TCP connections arriving on port 1234 to the Service named `bar-service`."

Depending on which ingress controller is in use, the actual way the user configures routing can vary significantly.

- Ingress controllers can always terminate and originate TLS connections (again, mostly focusing on HTTPS) to handle security at the edge of the cluster. This doesn't extend Linkerd's mTLS out to the ingress controller's clients; rather, it creates two separate domains in which TLS is operating and requires the ingress controller to translate between them, as shown in Figure 5-3.

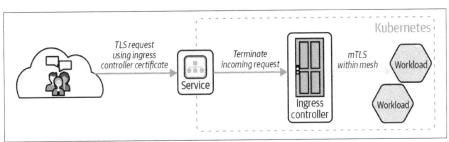

Figure 5-3. Ingress controllers and TLS

Keeping the two TLS worlds separate usually ends up making sense because the ingress controller needs to be presenting users with certificates that match what the user is expecting, but when its proxy interacts with Linkerd, it needs to present a properly crafted workload identity. These are not the same thing and shouldn't be conflated. Allowing the ingress controller to manage TLS with its client while allowing Linkerd to manage mTLS within the cluster is a powerful combination.

- Finally, many ingress controllers offer capabilities like end user authentication, circuit breaking, rate limiting, etc. These ingress controllers may also be called *API gateways*. An example of how one might handle end user authentication is shown in Figure 5-4.

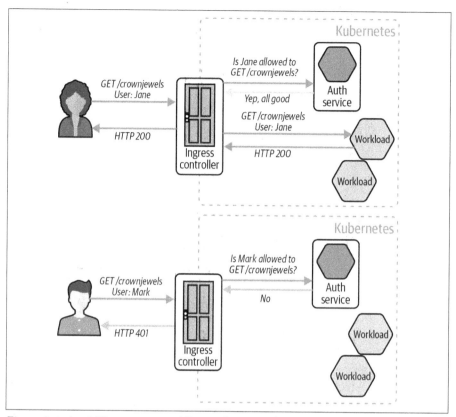

Figure 5-4. An API gateway providing end user authentication

API gateways have enormous latitude over what exactly happens to a user request, allowing very sophisticated capabilities indeed—though this is obviously out of scope for this book.

Ingress Controllers with Linkerd

Linkerd doesn't have a lot of constraints in terms of which ingress controller you use; almost any of them will work, usually without much trouble. From Linkerd's point of view, the ingress is just another meshed workload, and from the ingress controller's point of view, Linkerd is mostly invisible.

Ingress Controllers in Other Meshes

Some meshes take a very different approach here: they ship with an ingress controller that is tightly integrated with the mesh. Linkerd takes a very ingress-agnostic approach because it tends to increase flexibility, lessen operational complexity, and make it easier to adopt the ingress controller and the service mesh at different times.

The Ingress Controller Is Just Another Meshed Workload

From Linkerd's point of view, the ingress controller is mostly just a workload in the mesh, as shown in Figure 5-5. The fact that clients outside the cluster can talk to the ingress controller is really not something that Linkerd worries about: you still need to inject a sidecar into the ingress controller, and all the usual Linkerd features like mTLS and metrics just work.

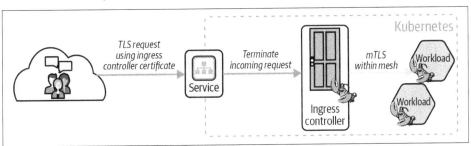

Figure 5-5. The ingress controller is just another workload

The single way that the ingress controller will almost always need special handling is that you'll almost always want to tell Linkerd to skip the ingress controller's incoming ports. This is because the ingress controller may need access to the client's IP address for routing or authorization purposes, but if Linkerd is handling the connection, then the only IP address the ingress controller will ever see is that of the Linkerd proxy. See Figure 5-6.

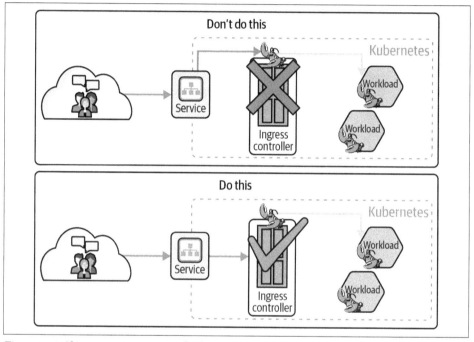

Figure 5-6. Skipping incoming traffic for the ingress controller

 Ingress Controllers Are Designed for the Edge

Remember that part of the job of an ingress controller is to sit at the edge of the cluster, so it already has to be designed to safely handle connections directly from the Internet. Telling Linkerd not to handle the incoming connections for the ingress controller shouldn't be any problem from a security point of view.

You'll use the `config.linkerd.io/skip-inbound-ports` annotation that we covered in Chapter 4 to skip the incoming ports. Pay attention to the port numbers—you need to skip the port(s) on which the ingress controller Pod is actually listening, which will often *not* be the port that the client uses! For example, if you associate your ingress controller with a Service like this one:

```
apiVersion: v1
kind: Service
metadata:
  name: myservice
spec:
  type: LoadBalancer
  ports:
  - name: http
    port: 80
    protocol: TCP
    targetPort: 8080
```

You'll need to skip inbound port 8080; trying to skip inbound port 80 would have no effect whatsoever. So, the correct annotation would be:

```
config.linkerd.io/skip-inbound-ports: 8080
```

Linkerd Is (Mostly) Invisible

From the point of view of the ingress controller, Linkerd is basically invisible. This is by design: adding Linkerd to a running application is meant to just work, after all! But there are two things to be aware of to make sure that everything is working as smoothly as possible: the ingress controller should use cleartext within the cluster, and it should route to Services rather than endpoints.

Use Cleartext Within the Cluster

We know: this is probably the only time in years you've seen anyone recommend using cleartext instead of TLS. To be clear, we're *not* talking about the connection from the client to the ingress controller! (Definitely use HTTPS for that.) Here, we're talking about the connections made from the ingress controller to meshed workloads in the cluster, as shown in Figure 5-7.

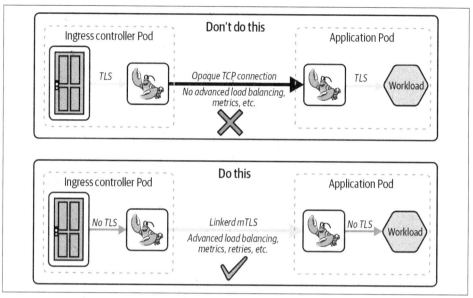

Figure 5-7. Let Linkerd handle mTLS inside the cluster

For those connections, you should use cleartext. If the ingress controller originates TLS to the workload, Linkerd can't do anything more than per-connection proxying; you miss out on per-request load balancing, proper request metrics, and a lot of other really useful things that Linkerd brings to the table. Using cleartext connections allows all the advanced functionality and is still safe because Linkerd's mTLS will protect the connection.

Route to Services, Not Endpoints

This is an area where Kubernetes nomenclature and concepts are particularly challenging. A Kubernetes Service actually has three entirely distinct parts, and all three are relevant for this point:

- The Service causes a name to appear in the cluster's DNS service.
- That DNS name is associated with a single IP address for the Service itself.
- The Service is also associated with a set of Pods, and each Pod has an IP address that is different from every other Pod's *and* from the Service's IP address.

Collectively, the IP addresses of the Pods are called the *endpoints* of the Service. (Kubernetes also has resources called Endpoints and EndpointSlices, but we're just talking about the set of Pod IP addresses for the moment.)

These parts are shown in Figure 5-8. Again, all three are relevant when considering service mesh routing.

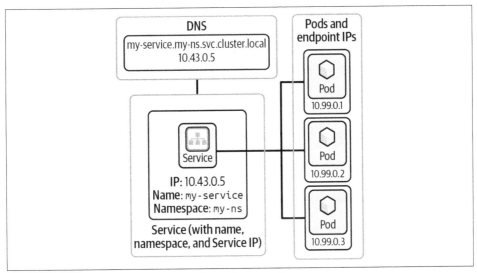

Figure 5-8. The three distinct parts of a Kubernetes Service

It matters which IP address the ingress controller uses for its connections because normally Linkerd will only load balance connections made to the Service's IP address, *not* connections made directly to an endpoint's IP address, as shown in Figure 5-9.

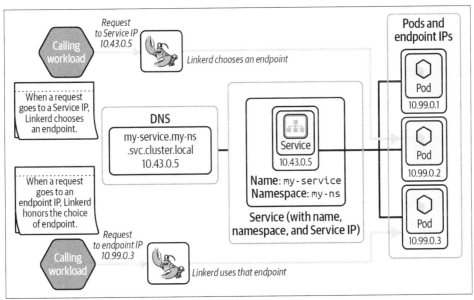

Figure 5-9. How Linkerd chooses where to route

Linkerd handles routing this way to maximize choice for the application designer: it's easy to have the ingress controller simply hand off all load balancing decisions to Linkerd (by routing to the Service IP), and it's still possible to have the ingress controller do its own load balancing (by routing directly to endpoint IPs).

In most common cases, having the ingress controller route to the Service IP is the simplest way to take full advantage of Linkerd.

Gateway API and Service Routing

Gateway API introduces a wrinkle into this recommendation: it will need to support cloud gateway controllers that aren't really running in the cluster and therefore can't have a Linkerd proxy running next to them. At the same time, these cloud gateway controllers can be extremely latency-sensitive, so they're less likely to support Service routing.

This is an area of active work within the GAMMA initiative and Gateway API as a whole.

Depending on which ingress controller you're using, you might need to specifically configure the ingress controller to do this—or you might find that it is not possible to configure your ingress controller to route to the Service IP. For these ingress controllers, you'll need to use Linkerd's *ingress mode*.

Ingress Mode

When ingress mode is active and Linkerd receives a request to an endpoint IP with the l5d-dst-override header set to a fully qualified Service DNS name, Linkerd will route the request as if it had gone to the Service IP address for the service named by the l5d-dst-override header, as shown in Figure 5-10.

For example, given a Service my-service in namespace my-ns, if you send a request directly to one of the endpoint IPs for my-service but set its l5d-dst-override header as shown here, then Linkerd will treat the connection as if it had been made to the Service IP for my-service:

```
l5d-dst-override: my-service.my-ns.svc.cluster.local
```

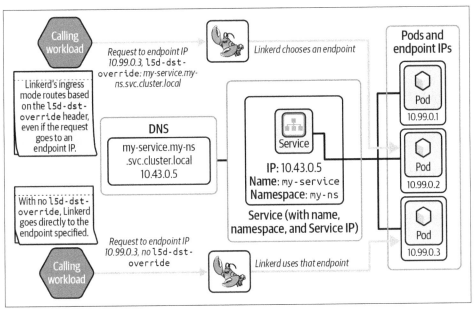

Figure 5-10. Linkerd ingress mode routing

The Ingress Controller Must Inject l5d-dst-override

To effectively use ingress mode, the ingress controller must inject the l5d-dst-override header into every request. An ingress controller that cannot inject this header is not compatible with Linkerd ingress mode. Linkerd cannot create the l5d-dst-override header itself, because in general, it's not possible to determine the name of a Service from one of its endpoint IP addresses. This is because a given Pod can be part of multiple Services.

If possible, it's usually better to configure the ingress controller to route to Services than to use ingress mode.

To use ingress mode, inject the proxy with:

```
linkerd.io/inject: ingress
```

rather than:

```
linkerd.io/inject: enabled
```

Specific Ingress Controller Examples

Here are some specific examples of configuring different ingress controllers for use with Linkerd. This is *not* an exhaustive list by any means—it's just a convenient set to show a fairly wide range of possibilities. The Linkerd ingress documentation (*https://oreil.ly/Nl7MR*) has more on this topic.

For our examples here, we'll take a look at Emissary-ingress, NGINX, and Envoy Gateway.

Emissary-ingress

Emissary-ingress (*https://oreil.ly/vHmjZ*) is an open source, Kubernetes-native API gateway that's been around since 2017. It's built on the Envoy proxy, focuses on operational simplicity and self-service configuration, and has been a CNCF incubating project since 2021. It defines its own native configuration CRDs but can also use Ingress resources or Gateway API. (Full disclosure: Flynn is the original author of Emissary.)

There's really not too much to dig into as far as setting up Emissary with Linkerd; it basically just works. Emissary defaults to routing to Services, so really the only thing to consider when adding Emissary to the Linkerd mesh is to skip Emissary's incoming ports if you need Emissary to know client IP addresses. And you'll want to make sure that Emissary isn't originating TLS to the workloads.

NGINX

NGINX is an open source API gateway and web server that was around long before Kubernetes came along. Though it's not a CNCF project itself, it served as the core of the `ingress-nginx` Kubernetes ingress controller (*https://oreil.ly/m-O2N*), which was one of the first ingress controllers using the Ingress resource, and it has been sufficiently popular for long enough that people generally mean `ingress-nginx` when they talk about running NGINX for Kubernetes.

By default, `ingress-nginx` will route to endpoint IPs, not Service IPs. To tell it to route to Service IPs instead, you'll need to include an `ingress-nginx` annotation on your Ingress resources:

```
nginx.ingress.kubernetes.io/service-upstream: "true"
```

Installing and meshing `ingress-nginx` after that should be painless. Remember to look at skipping incoming ports, too!

Envoy Gateway

As of this writing, Envoy Gateway has recently reached version 1.0. It provides an interesting opportunity to explore using Gateway API to manage both the ingress and the mesh in a Linkerd cluster.

Gateway API has the interesting characteristic that, by design, the user doesn't directly install the Pods that handle data (the data plane). Instead, the user installs a Gateway API control plane that understands how to watch Gateway resources. Then, when the user creates the Gateway, the Gateway API control plane creates the data plane Pods.

Envoy Gateway, as a Gateway API control plane, interprets this design characteristic to mean that whenever it sees a change to its Gateway resource, it actually deletes and re-creates the data plane Pods. This makes it a touch challenging to manage injecting the Envoy Gateway data plane into the mesh! The most effective way to handle this is to apply the `linkerd.io/inject` annotation to the `envoy-gateway-system` namespace, which is where the data plane Deployment will be created.

Also, Envoy Gateway always routes to endpoint IP addresses in version 1.0. Until this is resolved in a future release of Envoy Gateway, it limits Linkerd's ability to do advanced routing when using Envoy Gateway. (It's possible to mesh Envoy Gateway in ingress mode and then configure HTTPRoutes to inject the `l5d-dst-override` header, but it's a bit manual at present.)

Since Linkerd always gets to manage security though (including encryption and policy), Envoy Gateway with Linkerd is still a practical and interesting combination. Just pay attention to the incoming ports, as with the other ingress controllers!

Summary

One of Linkerd's strengths is its ability to work with a wide variety of ingress controllers. As long as a given ingress controller can accept the Linkerd sidecar and route to Services, it should work seamlessly with Linkerd. This leaves you free to choose whatever ingress controller works well for your team and your application and be confident that it'll get along with Linkerd.

# CHAPTER 6

The Linkerd CLI

The Linkerd command line interface (CLI) is a useful tool for interacting with the Linkerd control plane. The CLI can help you check on the health of a Linkerd instance, view details about proxies and certificates, troubleshoot aberrant behavior, and view policy. It is the recommended way to directly interface with Linkerd. It handles all the major tasks you'll need to work with your Linkerd installs and provides important tools for validating and examining Linkerd.

In this chapter, we'll cover some of the most useful things the CLI can do and illustrate how to take best advantage of it. The CLI is, of course, constantly evolving as new Linkerd releases come out, so it's always important to keep an eye on the official documentation (*https://oreil.ly/0GjuM*).

Installing the CLI

The CLI is versioned along with the rest of Linkerd, so when you install the CLI, you'll start by choosing which release channel to use.

To install from the stable channel, you'll refer to the vendor instructions (such as those for Buoyant Enterprise for Linkerd (*https://oreil.ly/6apOU*)).

To install completely open source Linkerd from the edge channel, you'll refer to the Linkerd quickstart (*https://oreil.ly/A3Lyl*). At the time of this writing, that boils down to:

```
$ curl --proto '=https' --tlsv1.2 -sSfL https://run.linkerd.io/install-edge | sh
```

In either case, once you install the CLI you'll need to add it to your PATH in the appropriate manner for your shell. For example, if you use bash you can alter the PATH variable directly:

```
$ export PATH=$HOME/.linkerd2/bin:$PATH
```

Updating the CLI

To update the CLI, just rerun the installation command. Over time, you'll end up with multiple versions stored locally, and you can choose among them.

Installing a Specific Version

Normally, the Linkerd CLI installer (for either channel) will install the most recent version of the CLI. You can force it to install a specific version by setting the LINKERD2_VERSION environment variable when you run the install script. For example, using the edge channel:

```
$ curl --proto '=https' --tlsv1.2 -sSfL https://run.linkerd.io/install-edge \
    | LINKERD2_VERSION="stable-2.13.12" sh
```

Set LINKERD2_VERSION for sh, Not curl

Pay attention to where the LINKERD2_VERSION environment variable is set in the preceding command: it needs to be set for the sh command executing the script that curl has downloaded, not for the curl command itself. Setting the environment variable for curl won't do anything.

Alternate Ways to Install

If you're on a Mac, Homebrew (*https://brew.sh*) is a simple way to install the CLI: just brew install linkerd. You can also download the CLI directly from the Linkerd releases page (*https://oreil.ly/vcUOa*).

Using the CLI

The CLI works broadly like any other Go CLI, such as kubectl:

```
$ linkerd command [options]
```

The *command* tells the CLI what exactly you want to do; the *options* are optional arguments to the specific command. You can always use the `--help` option to get help. For instance, `linkerd --help` will tell you what commands are available:

```
$ linkerd --help
linkerd manages the Linkerd service mesh.

Usage:
  linkerd [command]

Available Commands:
  authz        List authorizations for a resource
  check        Check the Linkerd installation for potential problems
  completion   Output shell completion code for the specified shell (bash, zsh
               or fish)
  diagnostics  Commands used to diagnose Linkerd components
  help         Help about any command
  identity     Display the certificate(s) of one or more selected pod(s)
  inject       Add the Linkerd proxy to a Kubernetes config
  install      Output Kubernetes configs to install Linkerd
  install-cni  Output Kubernetes configs to install Linkerd CNI
  jaeger       jaeger manages the jaeger extension of Linkerd service mesh
  multicluster Manages the multicluster setup for Linkerd
  profile      Output service profile config for Kubernetes
  prune        Output extraneous Kubernetes resources in the linkerd control
               plane
  uninject     Remove the Linkerd proxy from a Kubernetes config
  uninstall    Output Kubernetes resources to uninstall Linkerd control plane
  upgrade      Output Kubernetes configs to upgrade an existing Linkerd control
               plane
  version      Print the client and server version information
  viz          viz manages the linkerd-viz extension of Linkerd service mesh

Flags:
      --api-addr string            Override kubeconfig and communicate directly
                                   with the control plane at host:port (mostly
                                   for testing)
      --as string                  Username to impersonate for Kubernetes
                                   operations
      --as-group stringArray       Group to impersonate for Kubernetes
                                   operations
      --cni-namespace string       Namespace in which the Linkerd CNI plugin is
                                   installed (default "linkerd-cni")
      --context string             Name of the kubeconfig context to use
  -h, --help                       help for linkerd
      --kubeconfig string          Path to the kubeconfig file to use for CLI
                                   requests
  -L, --linkerd-namespace string   Namespace in which Linkerd is installed
                                   ($LINKERD_NAMESPACE) (default "linkerd")
      --verbose                    Turn on debug logging

Use "linkerd [command] --help" for more information about a command.
```

As this output shows, you can also get help on specific commands. For example, linkerd check --help will get help for the check command, as shown here:

```
$ linkerd check --help
Check the Linkerd installation for potential problems.

The check command will perform a series of checks to validate that the linkerd
CLI and control plane are configured correctly. If the command encounters a
failure it will print additional information about the failure and exit with a
non-zero exit code.

Usage:
  linkerd check [flags]

Examples:
  # Check that the Linkerd control plane is up and running
  linkerd check

  # Check that the Linkerd control plane can be installed in the "test"
  # namespace
  linkerd check --pre --linkerd-namespace test

  # Check that the Linkerd data plane proxies in the "app" namespace are up and
  # running
  linkerd check --proxy --namespace app

Flags:
      --cli-version-override string   Used to override the version of the cli
                                      (mostly for testing)
      --crds                          Only run checks which determine if the
                                      Linkerd CRDs have been installed
      --expected-version string       Overrides the version used when checking
                                      if Linkerd is running the latest version
                                      (mostly for testing)
  -h, --help                          help for check
      --linkerd-cni-enabled           When running pre-installation checks
                                      (--pre), assume the linkerd-cni plugin is
                                      already installed, and a NET_ADMIN check
                                      is not needed
  -n, --namespace string              Namespace to use for --proxy checks
                                      (default: all namespaces)
  -o, --output string                 Output format. One of: table, json, short
                                      (default "table")
      --pre                           Only run pre-installation checks, to
                                      determine if the control plane can be
                                      installed
      --proxy                         Only run data-plane checks, to determine
                                      if the data plane is healthy
      --wait duration                 Maximum allowed time for all tests to pass
                                      (default 5m0s)
```

```
Global Flags:
      --api-addr string             Override kubeconfig and communicate directly
                                    with the control plane at host:port (mostly
                                    for testing)
      --as string                   Username to impersonate for Kubernetes
                                    operations
      --as-group stringArray        Group to impersonate for Kubernetes
                                    operations
      --cni-namespace string        Namespace in which the Linkerd CNI plugin is
                                    installed (default "linkerd-cni")
      --context string              Name of the kubeconfig context to use
      --kubeconfig string           Path to the kubeconfig file to use for CLI
                                    requests
  -L, --linkerd-namespace string    Namespace in which Linkerd is installed
                                    ($LINKERD_NAMESPACE) (default "linkerd")
      --verbose                     Turn on debug logging
```

Selected Commands

The linkerd CLI supports a lot of commands. The official documentation (*https:// oreil.ly/M3qdg*), as always, has the full set; in this chapter, we're going to summarize some of the most broadly useful commands. These are the ones you should always have close to hand.

linkerd version

The first command to know about is linkerd version, which simply reports the running version of the linkerd CLI and (if possible) of the Linkerd control plane:

```
$ linkerd version
Client version: stable-2.14.6
Server version: stable-2.14.6
```

If you don't have Linkerd running in your cluster, linkerd version will show unavailable for the server version.

If linkerd version can't talk to your cluster, it will treat that as an error. You can use the --client option to just check the version of the CLI itself, without even trying to talk to the cluster, though:

```
$ linkerd version --client
Client version: stable-2.14.6
```

CLI Versions Versus Control Plane Versions

It's very important to remember that the CLI version is *independent* of the control plane version. Some CLI commands are quite complex and do a lot of subtle manipulations, so it's crucial to make sure that your CLI version matches your control plane version. A difference of one major version is OK, but more than one is not supported.

linkerd check

The `linkerd check` command gives an at-a-glance view of the health of Linkerd in your cluster. It will test for many known failure conditions and allow you to run extension-specific health checks. This deceptively simple command actually offers a lot of powerful tools for validating and checking the current state of your mesh.

The simplest—and most complete—way to use `linkerd check` is to run it with no arguments:

```
$ linkerd check
```

This will run a default set of checks that are both reasonably exhaustive and finish in a reasonable amount of time, including (in addition to quite a few other things):

- Making sure Linkerd is correctly installed in the default namespace
- Checking that Linkerd's certificates are valid
- Running checks for all installed extensions
- Double-checking necessary permissions

Running this command will give you a lot of insight into the current state of Linkerd in your cluster, and in fact if you need to file a bug report against Linkerd, you will *always* be asked to include the output of `linkerd check`.

linkerd check --pre

The precheck option runs a set of checks to make sure that your Kubernetes environment is ready to have Linkerd installed:

```
$ linkerd check --pre
```

This is the only use of `linkerd` check that does *not* require Linkerd to already be installed. The precheck makes sure both that your cluster meets the minimum technical requirements to run Linkerd and that you have appropriate permissions to perform a core Linkerd install. It is a useful part of preparing to install Linkerd on a new cluster.

> **Precheck and the CNI Plugin**
>
> If you plan on running Linkerd with the CNI plugin installed, you'll need to run `linkerd check --pre --linkerd-cni-enabled` so that `linkerd` check doesn't try to check for the `NET_ADMIN` capability.

linkerd check --proxy

You can also tell `linkerd` check to specifically check the data plane:

```
$ linkerd check --proxy
```

The proxy check runs many—though not all—of the checks performed by the basic `linkerd` check command. However, it also runs extra checks specific to the data plane, such as verifying that Linkerd proxies are running.

Linkerd extension checks

Each installed Linkerd extension has its own specific set of checks it will run during `linkerd` check. If needed, you can also run *only* the checks for a specific extension with `linkerd` *extension* check. For example, this is how you'd run only the checks for the Linkerd Viz extension:

```
$ linkerd viz check
```

> **Why Limit Checks?**
>
> Remember that `linkerd` check with no arguments will run the checks for all installed extensions. Limiting checks to a single extension is primarily helpful to reduce the amount of time that `linkerd` check takes to run.

Additional options for linkerd check

The `linkerd check` command obeys all the global CLI overrides, like changing the namespace in which you have Linkerd installed (`--namespace`) or modifying your KUBECONFIG (`--kubeconfig`) or Kubernetes context (`--context`). Additionally:

- `--output` allows you to specify the output type, which is useful if you want to override the default table output. Options include `json`, `basic`, `short`, and `table`. Outputting JSON can be particularly helpful if you intend to consume the check data programmatically.

- `--wait` overrides the amount of time the checks will wait in the event something isn't right. The default value is 5 minutes, which can be unnecessarily long in many cases.

linkerd inject

The `linkerd inject` command reads Kubernetes resources and outputs new versions that have been modified to add the Linkerd proxy container as appropriate. The `linkerd inject` command:

- Reads resources from its standard input, from local files, or from an HTTPS URL
- Can operate on multiple resources at once
- Knows to modify only Pods and leave other kinds of resources alone
- Allows you to configure the proxies as well
- Outputs the modified resources on its standard output, leaving the task of actually applying them to you

That last point is worth repeating: `linkerd inject` will never modify any of its sources directly. Instead, it outputs the modified Kubernetes resources so that you can apply them yourself, include them in a Git repo, or do whatever else is appropriate for your environment. This "output, don't overwrite" idiom is common across the entire `linkerd` CLI.

Using `linkerd inject` can be as simple as:

```
$ linkerd inject https://url.to/yml | kubectl apply -f -
```

As always, you can find more examples and see the full docs by running `linkerd inject --help`.

You Must Handle Applying Injected Resources

The most important thing to remember about `linkerd inject` is that it does not, in and of itself, make any changes to your cluster. You're always responsible for applying the output of the `linkerd` CLI to your cluster yourself, whether by simply feeding the output to `kubectl apply`, committing it so that GitOps takes over, or something else.

Injecting in ingress mode

The `--ingress` flag sets the ingress mode annotation for a workload. Before setting this flag, or the corresponding annotation, on your ingress, please verify that it is required. You can see the ingress docs (*https://oreil.ly/OgAej*) for more details on ingress mode.

Injecting manually

By default, `linkerd inject` just adds the `linkerd.io/inject` annotation to your workload Pods, trusting the proxy injector to do the heavy lifting. Setting the `--manual` flag instructs the CLI to add the sidecar container directly to your manifest, bypassing the proxy injector.

The `--manual` flag provides a valuable tool for overriding or modifying the proxy configuration in the event that you need to control something about the proxy that the usual configuration mechanisms don't support. Be careful when tampering with the proxy configuration directly, though, as you can quickly find yourself falling out of sync with your overall proxy configuration.

Injecting the debug sidecar

Setting `--enable-debug-sidecar` will add an annotation to your workload that will cause the proxy injector to add an additional debug sidecar to your Pods. Before trying to use the debug sidecar, you should definitely read Chapter 15 and the debug container documentation (*https://oreil.ly/CVc6-*).

linkerd identity

The `linkerd identity` command provides a useful tool for troubleshooting Pod certificates. It allows you to see the certificate details of any Pod or Pods; for example, here's how you can get the identity of a Pod belonging to the Linkerd destination controller:

```
$ linkerd identity -n linkerd linkerd-destination-7447d467f8-f4n9w
POD linkerd-destination-7447d467f8-f4n9w (1 of 1)

Certificate:
    Data:
        Version: 3 (0x2)
        Serial Number: 3 (0x3)
    Signature Algorithm: ECDSA-SHA256
        Issuer: CN=identity.linkerd.cluster.local
        Validity
            Not Before: Apr 5 13:51:13 2023 UTC
            Not After : Apr 6 13:51:53 2023 UTC
        Subject: CN=linkerd-destination.linkerd.serviceaccount.identity.link-
erd.cluster.local
        Subject Public Key Info:
            Public Key Algorithm: ECDSA
                Public-Key: (256 bit)
                X:
                    98:41:63:15:e1:0e:99:81:3c:ee:18:a5:55:fe:a5:
                    40:bd:cf:a2:cd:c2:e8:30:09:8c:8a:c6:8a:20:e7:
                    3c:cf
                Y:
                    53:7e:3c:05:d4:86:de:f9:89:cb:73:e9:37:98:08:
                    8f:e5:ec:39:c3:6c:c7:42:47:f0:ea:0a:c7:66:fe:
                    8d:a5
                Curve: P-256
        X509v3 extensions:
            X509v3 Key Usage: critical
                Digital Signature, Key Encipherment
            X509v3 Extended Key Usage:
                TLS Web Server Authentication, TLS Web Client Authentication
            X509v3 Authority Key Identifier:

keyid:37:C0:12:A1:AC:2D:A9:36:2D:35:83:6B:5C:99:9A:A2:5E:9C:E5:C5
            X509v3 Subject Alternative Name:
                DNS:linkerd-destination.linkerd.serviceaccount.identity.link-
erd.cluster.local

    Signature Algorithm: ECDSA-SHA256
        30:45:02:20:4a:fb:02:db:17:e7:df:64:a4:7b:d2:08:a2:2e:
        66:e5:a4:74:14:35:d5:1a:f7:fc:15:95:9b:73:60:dd:78:a4:
        02:21:00:8c:12:fb:bf:80:7a:c4:25:91:0c:ac:03:37:ca:e0:
        82:d5:9d:9b:54:f1:20:b0:f0:14:e0:ef:ae:a8:ba:70:00
```

Your Pod Identities Will Be Different

If you try this command, your Pod ID—and the specific certificate information—will be different. However, none of the information provided by `linkerd identity` is sensitive; it only shows public information. It's always safe to run.

You can use the output of this command to check the validity of a given Pod certificate. It also gives you the details of what authority signed the certificate, so you can check that it is signed by the correct intermediary and root CAs.

linkerd diagnostics

The `linkerd diagnostics` command is a powerful tool that enables platform operators to gather information directly from Linkerd. It will allow you to directly scrape details from the metrics endpoints of the various Linkerd components.

This command also allows you to diagnose hard-to-identify conditions, like Linkerd's failfast error, by listing out the endpoints for a given service. Some examples are given here; see also the latest documentation (*https://oreil.ly/egNPA*) on the Linkerd site.

Gathering metrics

The `linkerd diagnostics` command can gather data directly from the metrics endpoints of the control plane and data plane. To gather control plane metrics, use this command:

```
$ linkerd diagnostics controller-metrics
#
# POD linkerd-destination-8498c6764f-96tqr (1 of 5)
# CONTAINER destination
#
# HELP cluster_store_size The number of linked clusters in the remote discove...
# TYPE cluster_store_size gauge
cluster_store_size 0
# HELP endpoint_profile_updates_queue_overflow A counter incremented whenever...
# TYPE endpoint_profile_updates_queue_overflow counter
endpoint_profile_updates_queue_overflow 0
# HELP endpoint_updates_queue_overflow A counter incremented whenever the end...
# TYPE endpoint_updates_queue_overflow counter
endpoint_updates_queue_overflow{service="kubernetes.default.svc.cluster.local...
# HELP endpoints_cache_size Number of items in the client-go endpoints cache
# TYPE endpoints_cache_size gauge
endpoints_cache_size{cluster="local"} 17
...
```

To gather metrics data for a given proxy or set of proxies, use a command like the following:

```
$ linkerd diagnostics proxy-metrics -n emojivoto deploy/web
#
# POD web-5b97875957-xn269 (1 of 1)
#
# HELP inbound_http_authz_allow_total The total number of inbound HTTP reques...
# TYPE inbound_http_authz_allow_total counter
inbound_http_authz_allow_total{target_addr="0.0.0.0:4191",target_ip="0.0.0.0"...
inbound_http_authz_allow_total{target_addr="0.0.0.0:4191",target_ip="0.0.0.0"...
# HELP identity_cert_expiration_timestamp_seconds Time when the this proxy's ...
# TYPE identity_cert_expiration_timestamp_seconds gauge
identity_cert_expiration_timestamp_seconds 1705071458
# HELP identity_cert_refresh_count The total number of times this proxy's mTL...
# TYPE identity_cert_refresh_count counter
identity_cert_refresh_count 1
# HELP request_total Total count of HTTP requests.
# TYPE request_total counter
request_total{direction="inbound",target_addr="0.0.0.0:4191",target_ip="0.0.0...
request_total{direction="inbound",target_addr="0.0.0.0:4191",target_ip="0.0.0...
...
```

linkerd diagnostics produces raw Prometheus metrics, so you'll need to already have a sense of what information you're looking for if you're using these commands. Also note that the sample output has been truncated for space reasons—these commands produce *much* more output than what's shown here (hundreds of lines, or more, is typical).

Checking for endpoints

One of the hardest problems to debug in Linkerd tends to be when the linkerd2-proxy emits a message indicating it's in a *failfast* state. The failfast state is discussed in more detail in Chapter 15, but a very common reason to land in failfast is that a given service doesn't have any valid endpoints. You can check for this condition with linkerd diagnostics endpoints. For example, here we examine the endpoints for the emoji-svc service of the emojivoto sample application (*https://oreil.ly/ZnYsL*):

```
$ linkerd diagnostics endpoints emoji-svc.emojivoto.svc.cluster.local:8080
NAMESPACE    IP          PORT  POD                    SERVICE
emojivoto    10.42.0.15  8080  emoji-5b97875957-xn269  emoji-svc.emojivoto
```

Note that you must provide the fully qualified DNS name of the service as well as a port number. If no valid endpoints are found, linkerd diagnostics endpoints will report No endpoints found and, importantly, requests to the service will land in failfast.

Diagnosing policy

As of Linkerd 2.13, there is a new linkerd diagnostics policy command that can provide insight into Linkerd's advanced routing policy engine. For example, you can look at the policy applied to traffic on port 80 of the smiley Service in the faces namespace (as you might find if you're running the Faces demo application (*https://oreil.ly/a4OnB*)):

```
$ linkerd diagnostics policy -n faces svc/smiley 80 > smiley-diag.json
```

The output of `linkerd diagnostics policy` is *extremely* verbose JSON, so it's almost always a good idea to redirect it to a file as we've done here (or to `less`, `bat`, or a similar tool). You'll see sections for `http1.1`, `http2`, etc., and in each section will be a very detailed—and, again, verbose—breakdown of the policy being applied.

As an example, you might see output like that in Example 6-1 to describe what will happen to HTTP/2 traffic with no advanced policy applied.

Example 6-1. HTTP/2 output block without advanced policy

```
http2:
  routes:
  - metadata:
      Kind:
        Default: http
    rules:
    - backends:
        Kind:
          FirstAvailable:
            backends:
            - backend:
                Kind:
                  Balancer:
                    Load:
                      PeakEwma:
                        decay:
                          seconds: 10
                        default_rtt:
                          nanos: 30000000
                    discovery:
                      Kind:
                        Dst:
                          path: smiley.faces.svc.cluster.local:80
                metadata:
                  Kind:
                    Default: service
                queue:
                  capacity: 100
                  failfast_timeout:
                    seconds: 3
      matches:
      - path:
          Kind:
            Prefix: /
```

Alternatively, suppose that you apply the HTTPRoute resource shown in Example 6-2 to split traffic sent to smiley so that half the traffic proceeds to the smiley workload, and the other half is redirected to smiley2. (HTTPRoutes are discussed in more detail in Chapter 9.)

Example 6-2. HTTPRoute traffic splitting

```
apiVersion: policy.linkerd.io/v1beta3
kind: HTTPRoute
metadata:
  name: smiley-split
  namespace: faces
spec:
  parentRefs:
    - name: smiley
      kind: Service
      group: core
      port: 80
  rules:
  - backendRefs:
    - name: smiley
      port: 80
      weight: 50
    - name: smiley2
      port: 80
      weight: 50
```

With that HTTPRoute in effect, linkerd diagnostics policy might produce an http2 block like the one in Example 6-3, showing that traffic is indeed being split.

Example 6-3. HTTP/2 output block with traffic splitting

```
http2:
  routes:
  - metadata:
      Kind:
        Resource:
          group: policy.linkerd.io
          kind: HTTPRoute
          name: smiley-split
          namespace: faces
    rules:
    - backends:
        Kind:
          RandomAvailable:
            backends:
            - backend:
                backend:
                  Kind:
```

```
              Balancer:
                Load:
                  PeakEwma:
                    decay:
                      seconds: 10
                    default_rtt:
                      nanos: 30000000
                  discovery:
                    Kind:
                      Dst:
                        path: smiley.faces.svc.cluster.local:80
            metadata:
              Kind:
                Resource:
                  group: core
                  kind: Service
                  name: smiley
                  namespace: faces
                  port: 80
            queue:
              capacity: 100
              failfast_timeout:
                seconds: 3
        weight: 50
    - backend:
        backend:
          Kind:
            Balancer:
              Load:
                PeakEwma:
                  decay:
                    seconds: 10
                  default_rtt:
                    nanos: 30000000
                discovery:
                  Kind:
                    Dst:
                      path: smiley2.faces.svc.cluster.local:80
          metadata:
            Kind:
              Resource:
                group: core
                kind: Service
                name: smiley2
                namespace: faces
                port: 80
          queue:
            capacity: 100
            failfast_timeout:
              seconds: 3
        weight: 50
    matches:
```

```
- path:
    Kind:
      Prefix: /
```

As Linkerd evolves, this output will change, so take these examples with a grain of salt. The point of `linkerd diagnostics policy` is to provide sufficient detail that you can understand how Linkerd will manage traffic to a particular workload, no matter what changes are made to the source.

Summary

The `linkerd` CLI provides more than just the tooling you need to install Linkerd. It gives you critical operational tools that simplify the process of running Linkerd in your clusters. While it's definitely possible to use Linkerd and never run the `linkerd` CLI, the CLI is the most straightforward, effective way to deal with many real-world situations.

mTLS, Linkerd, and Certificates

Moving from a monolithic application to a microservices application puts us in a very interesting position as far as security is concerned. Where the monolith provided a natural security perimeter at the edge of its process, a microservices application has no natural security perimeter at all. Sensitive information that was previously protected by being passed in a function call inside the process now has to be sent over the network, as shown in Figure 7-1.

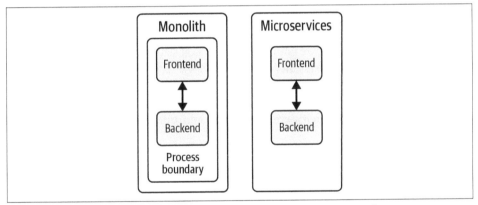

Figure 7-1. Security stance in a monolithic versus a microservices application

Additionally, the microservices are often running on infrastructure and network resources provided by outside teams, organizations, or even companies. If nothing is done to counter the threat, it's all too easy for an attacker with access to the network to read, intercept, and modify communications between microservices. This is obviously a serious problem.

Finally, the network doesn't even provide any secure way for a given microservice to know who made a call to it. The called microservice can find out the caller's IP and

MAC addresses, but these aren't actually secure—it's very easy to spoof the sender's IP address, for example. Things just get worse when the application is running on a network it doesn't control.

Secure Communications

To allow any microservices application to work, we need *secure communications*. There are three distinct elements to truly secure communications:

Authenticity
> We must be confident that we are talking to who we think we're talking to.

Confidentiality
> We must be confident that no one can read the data being sent over the connection.

Integrity
> We must be confident that our messages haven't been altered in transit.

These aren't new problems, and many different techniques have evolved to address them in various ways. Linkerd relies on one of the most trusted of these: *mutual TLS*, or *mTLS*.

TLS and mTLS

TLS, defined by RFC 8446 (*https://oreil.ly/K6Wwg*), is a battle-tested, industry-standard mechanism for secure communications that dates back to 1999. It's the same mechanism that web browsers have used for years to securely communicate with banks, shopping sites, etc. The modern Internet has been relying on TLS for nearly 25 years, and cryptanalysts have being trying for at least that long to find weaknesses in it. TLS provides authenticity, confidentiality, and integrity using the architecture shown in Figure 7-2.

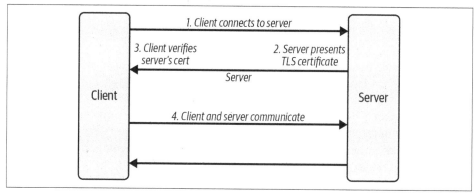

Figure 7-2. TLS architecture

(Linkerd specifically uses TLS version 1.3, but all TLS versions have used the same architecture.)

TLS ensures confidentiality by encrypting data in transit and integrity by adding message digests—cryptographic checksums—so that the receiver can validate that the data sent hasn't been altered. This takes care of two of our three concerns.

Authenticity is more complex. TLS uses *certificates* to cryptographically allow validating the identity of both the sender and the receiver. The TLS standard always requires the receiving end to identify itself by sending a certificate. In many cases, this is all that's needed; for example, when you use your web browser to visit a shopping site, it's not terribly useful for your browser to send a certificate since the shopping site will require you to log in separately.

For a service mesh, though, we need to authenticate both ends of the connection. This means we require both ends to send certificates for identification. When we use TLS like this (as Linkerd does), we call it mutual TLS or mTLS to distinguish it from the case where only the receiver identifies itself. This is shown in Figure 7-3.

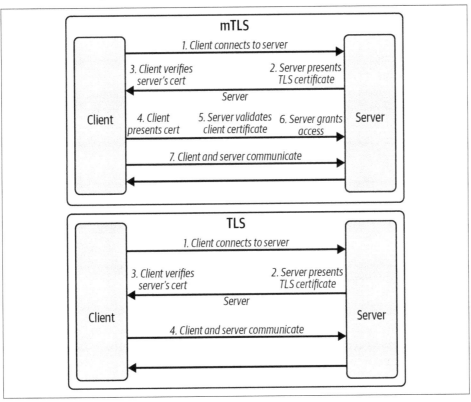

Figure 7-3. TLS compared to mTLS

Using certificates in both directions lets mTLS build on the guarantees provided by TLS: it provides a cryptographically validated identity of the client as well as the server, while still maintaining encryption in transit. For Linkerd, this means that mTLS guarantees that your workloads know whom they're talking to and that no third party will be able to intercept or listen in on their communication.

mTLS and Certificates

As we first discussed in Chapter 2, the certificates that mTLS relies on are built on keypairs consisting of a public key and a private key. The private key (of course) needs to be kept private: only the entity that the keypair identifies can know it. The public key, on the other hand, should be widely distributed: it's what allows verifying the identity of the entity holding the private key, so everyone who needs to communicate with that entity needs the public key.

Certificates give us a way to associate a *name* and other metadata with the keypair, which is useful because it allows us humans to more easily work with the certificate. They also give us a way for one certificate to attest that another is valid (*signing* or *issuing* a certificate), which is useful because it makes it much simpler to determine whether or not we trust a certificate.

Using certificates to sign other certificates creates a *trust hierarchy*, as shown in Figure 7-4. This hierarchy is important: mTLS can know that a certificate is valid as long as it has access to any of the public keys higher up in the hierarchy, and systems built on mTLS (including Linkerd) take advantage of this property.

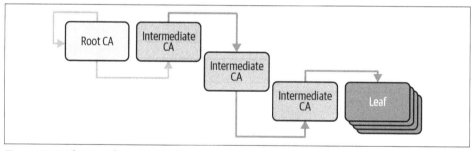

Figure 7-4. The certificate trust hierarchy

Finally, it's important to limit the lifespan of a given keypair: the longer a key is used, the greater the danger if it's compromised. Every so often, we need to replace the keys in use for a given certificate. This involves creating a new keypair, then generating a new certificate, and finally getting it properly signed. This entire process is called *rotating* the certificate; it is the main source of operational complexity when working with certificates.

Linkerd and mTLS

Linkerd transparently adds mTLS to all of your interapplication communications. This means that all meshed traffic is protected against interception and tampering. It also means your workloads can be certain of which workloads they're communicating with at all times.

This can only work if every meshed workload has a valid TLS certificate associated with that workload, and if all these *workload certificates* are part of the same trust hierarchy. Managing this by hand would be incredibly difficult, so Linkerd helps to automate it.

We talked about adding workloads to the mesh in Chapter 4, but let's revisit that in a bit more detail. When a workload is added to the mesh, it gets a linkerd2-proxy container added to its Pod. That container will be configured to intercept all TCP traffic going into and out of the Pod, and it will always attempt to build an mTLS session when a connection is made with another Pod. If the other Pod also has a linkerd2-proxy—meaning that it's part of the mesh!—then the connection will be protected with mTLS.

Since this mTLS connection happens from proxy to proxy, the application containers within the Pods never even know that mTLS is happening: from an application perspective, all communications between Pods look like they're using cleartext. This means that the application Pods don't see any information about the certificates that Linkerd is using, which in turn means that they don't need any special code to handle certificate information.

Protocol Detection and the Proxy

The fact that the proxy intercepts *all* communication between Pods means that you may sometimes need to give it extra information about the protocol, or indeed not try to do mTLS. This is all covered at some length in Chapter 4, but a good rule of thumb is that as long as the client speaks first, you're probably OK. If the server speaks first, you'll need to do some configuration.

Of course, that's only true if the server is in the mesh! If you're trying to communicate from a meshed Pod to an unmeshed Pod, you will always need to tell Linkerd to skip the traffic: it won't be able to do mTLS without the destination Pod being part of the mesh.

Certificates and Linkerd

We talked about Linkerd certificates back in Chapter 3. In this section, we'll go into more detail about exactly what these certificates are used for, how they are created, and what needs to happen when you want to rotate them. We're going to cover the three tiers of certificates used in Linkerd: trust anchor, identity issuer, and workload certificates.

From Linkerd's point of view, trust starts with its trust anchor certificate, as shown in Figure 7-5. The trust anchor can, of course, be signed by some other higher-level certificate—as far as Linkerd is concerned, though, trust stops with the trust anchor.

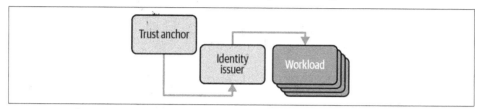

Figure 7-5. The Linkerd trust hierarchy

Linkerd automatically handles the generation, distribution, and rotation of workload certificates, while relying on the user to manage the trust anchor and the identity issuer. This is shown in Figure 7-6.

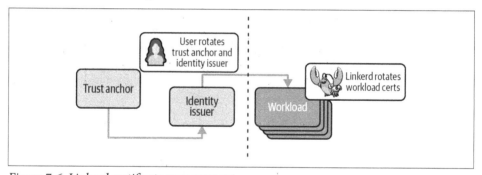

Figure 7-6. Linkerd certificate management

Never Let Your Certificates Expire

Because Linkerd requires mTLS connections between Pods by default, the health and security of the certificates it uses are absolutely critical to the healthy operation of the mesh—and thus your platform. If certificates expire, or can't be generated for new Pods, *you will incur downtime.*

This is the most common cause of downtime in production Linkerd clusters. Understanding and monitoring your Linkerd certificates is vital.

The Linkerd Trust Anchor

The Linkerd *trust anchor* is the certificate that provides the foundation for all trust in your cluster. It is used for exactly two things:

- When installing Linkerd, you will use the trust anchor to issue the Linkerd identity issuer certificate, which we'll discuss in the next section. This requires access to both the private and public keys of the trust anchor and is something done outside of Linkerd, before installation.

- Whenever a workload makes an mTLS connection to another workload, both workloads use the identity issuer and the trust anchor to verify the identity of the other workload. This requires access to only the public key of the trust anchor and happens constantly while the mesh is operating.

Since only the public key is needed for in-cluster operations (the second bullet in the preceding list), we recommend that you never store your trust anchor's private key in your Kubernetes cluster. Instead, store the trust anchor in a secure system outside of Kubernetes and only copy its public key into the cluster, as we'll cover in this chapter.

One very important thing to realize is that the trust anchor is not intrinsically tied to a cluster: it is completely independent of network topology or cluster boundaries. This means that if you give multiple clusters the same trust anchor, they'll be able to do secure mTLS between workloads in different clusters, as shown in Figure 7-7. This is extremely powerful, as it makes multicluster meshes very easy to set up.

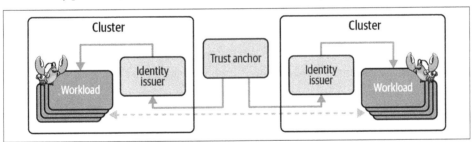

Figure 7-7. Multicluster trust hierarchy

Correspondingly, two clusters that should *not* be able to communicate with each other should *not* share a trust anchor! For most organizations, this implies not sharing trust anchors across environment tiers—that is, test clusters shouldn't have the same trust anchor as development or production clusters.

The Linkerd Identity Issuer

At the second level of the Linkerd trust hierarchy is the identity issuer certificate, as we also briefly touched on in Chapter 3. The identity issuer is used by the

Linkerd control plane's identity controller to issue workload certificates, as shown in Figure 7-8. Since the identity issuer is used to sign certificates, Linkerd must have access to both the private and public keys of the identity issuer certificate, which means that it must be stored in a Secret in the cluster.

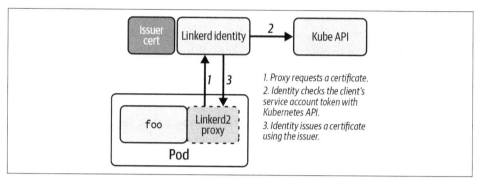

Figure 7-8. The issuer certificate and the identity controller

The identity issuer must be signed by the trust anchor, and since it must be stored in the cluster, each cluster must have its own identity issuer.

Linkerd Cannot Warn You If You Share Identity Issuer Certificates

There isn't any good way for Linkerd to warn you if you accidentally use the same identity issuer certificate in two clusters, and in fact everything will work. *Don't do this*, though. If you do, the two clusters will become indistinguishable, and an evildoer will potentially be able to use one cluster to create a workload certificate that can bypass authorization policy in the other cluster.

Make sure that each cluster has a unique identity issuer.

Linkerd Workload Certificates

Finally, we come to the certificates that actually do the work of providing mTLS between our applications. When a workload is added to a Linkerd mesh, the Linkerd proxy associated with each workload Pod automatically requests a workload certificate from the Linkerd identity controller. This workload certificate is the basis for the workload's identity. It will be signed by the identity issuer certificate, and since every other workload has access to the public keys of the identity issuer and the trust anchor, the validity of the workload certificate can be verified all the way back to the trust anchor.

The workload certificate for each Pod is cryptographically linked to the Kubernetes ServiceAccount assigned to the Pod, and its name includes the name of the Service-Account and the namespace. This allows your Pods to be uniquely identified when they communicate with each other. It also provides us with the identity we will need later when we build policy. The basic format for the identity name is:

`$serviceAccountName.$namespace.serviceaccount.identity.linkerd.$clusterDomain`

where `$clusterDomain` will be `cluster.local` if you haven't overridden it. (Most single-cluster Linkerd installations won't need to override this.)

Linkerd handles workload certificates completely automatically; you should never need to worry about managing them.

Certificate Lifetimes and Rotation

As we mentioned earlier, the longer you use a given key, the more valuable it tends to be to break that key. For this reason, certificates are given fixed lifespans, and they must be replaced before they expire. Replacing a certificate with a new one is called *rotating* the certificate.

Choosing exactly how often to rotate certificates is a balancing act. Rotating very frequently is most secure, but it can disrupt normal operations and require an impractical amount of effort. Rotating very infrequently—or not at all—is very simple, but also very insecure.

Linkerd handles rotating workload certificates for you: by default, workload certificates expire every 24 hours. However, rotating the identity issuer and trust anchor certificates is left up to you, since your organization's policy will often dictate how often you'll be rotating. The critical things to consider are:

Every time you rotate the trust anchor, you must also rotate the identity issuer.
> This is because the trust anchor must sign the identity issuer. If you've just generated a new trust anchor, there's no way the old identity issuer can be signed by the new trust anchor, so you need a new identity issuer too.
>
> In turn, this means that you *cannot* rotate the trust anchor more often than the identity issuer.

Every time you rotate the identity issuer, you may also rotate the workload certificates.
> Since workload certificates are automatically rotated by Linkerd, when you rotate the identity issuer you can opt to just wait for Linkerd to rotate the workload certificates. If you want to be sure they're rotated immediately, just restart the workloads.

The way you rotate a certificate depends on which certificate it is:

Rotating the trust anchor
> Rotating the trust anchor is actually out of scope for this book: in practice, if you adhere to the principle that clusters themselves should be ephemeral, it can be more practical to simply have the lifespan of the trust anchor mirror that of the

cluster. You can find more about rotating the trust anchor in the official Linkerd docs (*https://oreil.ly/9fAPV*).

Rotating the identity issuer

Rotating the identity issuer is a basic operational task in Linkerd. Ideally, you'll automate rotating the identity issuer with a tool like Venafi's cert-manager (*https://cert-manager.io*), and we show how to do this in this chapter. You can also manually rotate the trust anchor using the procedure shown in the official Linkerd docs (*https://oreil.ly/CN9IB*).

Whether you automate identity issuer rotation or do it manually, it is critical that you practice rotating the identity issuer *before* the identity issuer expires. Having a mechanism that you've never tested can be worse than not having anything set up at all.

Rotating the workload certificates

Workload certificates are automatically rotated by the Linkerd control plane, so you should almost never need to deal with them. (As noted previously, if you *do* want to rotate a workload certificate, just restart the workload.)

By default, workload certificates are valid for 24 hours, and the control plane will begin attempting to rotate a workload certificate once it's hit 70% of its effective lifetime.

Tuning Workload Certificates

If needed, you can tune the lifespan of workload certificates by setting the `issuanceLifetime` value when installing Linkerd, but recognize that there are two important operational concerns if you reduce this value.

First, you increase the frequency with which your Pods communicate with the identity controller, which increases the load on the identity controller.

Second, you reduce the amount of time you have to address problems with renewals. The proxy will begin attempting to renew at 70% of the lifespan: for a 24-hour lifespan, this means it will start trying with about 7 hours to go before the certificate expires, giving you about 7 hours to solve any problems that come up. If the whole lifespan is just 2 hours, you'll only have about half an hour to work with if anything goes wrong.

As you have likely surmised, we've only skimmed the surface of how certificates work in general, and in Linkerd in particular, but you should now have more than enough information to understand how certificates are used in Linkerd.

Certificate Management in Linkerd

It should be clear at this point that certificate management is a critical part of securing a production Linkerd installation. Properly managing certificates is an important way to reduce the likelihood of an incident. It can also help minimize time to recovery and the overall impact if something does go wrong.

With that in mind, our recommendations for everyone using Linkerd for any kind of production use are:

Couple the life of the trust anchor to the life of the cluster.
It's definitely possible to rotate the trust anchor, but treating the entire cluster as ephemeral and periodically rotating the whole cluster tends to make disaster recovery and provider migration ultimately simpler.

Automate rotating the identity issuer.
It's definitely possible to manage the identity issuer by hand, but we *strongly* recommend using a tool like cert-manager to regularly rotate the identity issuer certificate every few days instead. This shorter lifespan for the identity issuer can dramatically limit the scope of any incident, and using cert-manager makes it almost unnoticeable.

Automatic Certificate Management with cert-manager

Venafi's cert-manager is a CNCF project that manages automatic certificate generation and rotation, as shown in Figure 7-9. We're not going to cover the detailed inner workings of cert-manager (that's beyond the scope of this book); instead, we're going to focus on the concepts required to understand how to use cert-manager with Linkerd.

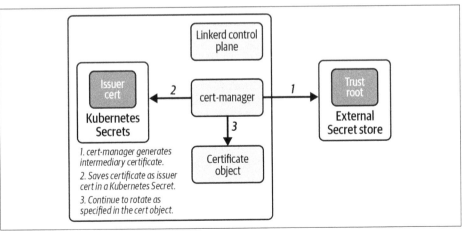

Figure 7-9. Automatic issuer certificate rotation with cert-manager

Installing cert-manager

We start by installing cert-manager using Helm to manage our install, as shown in Example 7-1. To follow along, you'll need the following tools available in your environment:

- kubectl
- k3d or another tool for getting a local Kubernetes cluster
- helm3

Example 7-1. Installing cert-manager

```
# Start by creating the cluster
$ k3d cluster create luar

# Add the jetstack Helm repo if you don't already have it
$ helm repo add jetstack https://charts.jetstack.io

# Make sure your Helm repositories are up-to-date
$ helm repo update

# Install cert-manager
$ helm install \
  cert-manager jetstack/cert-manager \
  --namespace cert-manager \
  --create-namespace \
  --version v1.12.0 \
  --set installCRDs=true

# Check out your cert-manager Pods
$ kubectl get pods -n cert-manager
```

Software Versions

Be aware that our examples are using specific versions to make sure that things work at the time of this writing. There may be more updated versions available by the time you read this, though; make sure you're using appropriate versions.

Configuring cert-manager for Linkerd

While a deep dive into cert-manager is out of scope for this book, it's definitely worth discussing its overall architecture for our use case. cert-manager is configured with Issuer and Certificate resources: an Issuer resource tells cert-manager where to find the keys it needs to issue a certificate, and a Certificate resource tells cert-manager which Issuer to use for a specific certificate.

In our case, as shown in Figure 7-9, we'll create an Issuer that holds the trust anchor keys and a Certificate that describes how to use that Issuer to get a Linkerd issuer certificate.

We mentioned at the beginning of the chapter that you never want to add your root CA's private key to your Kubernetes cluster. Because standing up an external key store is out of scope for this book, we're going to break that rule in Example 7-2 and use cert-manager with the trust anchor stored in a Kubernetes Secret. In any real production environment you would *not* do this, but the overall setup will stay the same, with one Issuer and one Certificate: you'll just change the Issuer definition to use your external agent instead. (cert-manager supports many different external agents; see the documentation (*https://oreil.ly/f5354*).)

> **Keep the Trust Anchor Key out of the Cluster!**
>
> Again, *do not* use this setup in production. It can be made safer, but having your trust anchor's secret key in the cluster will never be as safe as having it exist only in an external store.

Example 7-2. Generating certificates for Linkerd

```
# Start by generating a trust anchor for the cluster.
$ step certificate create root.linkerd.cluster.local ca.crt ca.key \
  --profile root-ca --no-password --insecure --not-after=87600h

# Create the linkerd namespace so that we have a place to install
# the trust anchor Secret.
$ kubectl create ns linkerd

# Save the trust anchor as a Secret in the linkerd namespace.
#
# During your real-world installs, you'd instead use an external
# cert-manager-compatible Secret store (like Vault) to store the
# trust anchor.
$ kubectl create secret tls linkerd-trust-anchor \
  --cert=ca.crt \
  --key=ca.key \
  --namespace=linkerd

# Create a cert-manager Issuer that uses the trust anchor Secret
# to issue certificates. This Issuer must be in the same namespace
# as the trust anchor Secret.
#
# During your real-world installs, you'd instead change this
# Issuer to connect to your external Secret store.
$ kubectl apply -f - <<EOF
apiVersion: cert-manager.io/v1
kind: Issuer
metadata:
  name: linkerd-trust-anchor
  namespace: linkerd
spec:
  ca:
    secretName: linkerd-trust-anchor
EOF
```

```
# With the Issuer created, we will now use a Certificate to instruct
# cert-manager to create our identity issuer certificate. We will
# also instruct it to automatically rotate that certificate every 48
# hours. This Certificate must be in the same namespace as the Secret
# it is writing, which (again) is the linkerd namespace.
$ kubectl apply -f - <<EOF
apiVersion: cert-manager.io/v1
kind: Certificate
metadata:
  name: linkerd-identity-issuer
  namespace: linkerd
spec:
  secretName: linkerd-identity-issuer
  duration: 48h
  issuerRef:
    name: linkerd-trust-anchor
    kind: Issuer
  commonName: identity.linkerd.cluster.local
  dnsNames:
  - identity.linkerd.cluster.local
  isCA: true
  privateKey:
    algorithm: ECDSA
  usages:
  - cert sign
  - crl sign
  - server auth
  - client auth
EOF
```

Let's go back over what we just did. We started by installing cert-manager into our cluster, which will automate the process of issuing and rotating certificates. We then created a trust anchor and told cert-manager to use that certificate to automatically create and rotate Linkerd's issuer certificate. The issuer certificate is an intermediary CA that Linkerd will use to create, distribute, and rotate the individual workload certificates. cert-manager will rotate the issuer certificate every 48 hours, as we defined in its Certificate object.

Let's take a quick tour around our cluster, as shown in Example 7-3, to see what cert-manager will actually do with this setup.

Example 7-3. Looking around

```
# First, let's validate that the trust anchor Secret exists and
# has some information in it.
$ kubectl get secret linkerd-trust-anchor -n linkerd

# Given that, we can use the step CLI to examine the public part
# of the certificate itself. The way this works is that the public
# part is stored, base-64 encoded, in the "tls.crt" key of the
# Secret, so we extract that, decode it, and hand it to step.
$ kubectl get secret linkerd-trust-anchor -n linkerd \
    -o jsonpath='{.data.tls\.crt}' \
    | base64 -d \
    | step certificate inspect -

# Next, let's check to see if cert-manager was able to create
# our issuer certificate. We should see a Certificate named
# linkerd-identity-issuer with a "ready" status of True.
$ kubectl get certificate -n linkerd

# Following that, we'll check in on the identity issuer Secret.
# This is just like what we did for the trust anchor, with a
# different name for the Secret.
$ kubectl get secret linkerd-identity-issuer -n linkerd \
    -o jsonpath='{.data.tls\.crt}' \
    | base64 -d \
    | step certificate inspect -
```

With that out of the way, we can now install Linkerd.

Installing Linkerd using cert-manager

Once cert-manager is set up to issue certs, we need to install Linkerd so that it knows to use the certificates that cert-manager is managing, as shown in Figure 7-9.

You'll remember that in Chapter 3 we went through the various ways to install Linkerd. We'll use Helm for our installation, as shown in Example 7-4, since we recommend that folks hoping to run Linkerd in production install Linkerd with Helm.

Example 7-4. Installing Linkerd with cert-manager

```
# Configure our Linkerd Helm repo.
$ helm repo add linkerd https://helm.linkerd.io/stable

# Update our repos.
$ helm repo update

# Install the Linkerd CRDs.
$ helm install linkerd-crds -n linkerd --version 1.6.1 linkerd/linkerd-crds

# Install Linkerd's control plane.
#
# Unlike in earlier chapters, this install will not have us specifying
# the issuer certificate. Instead, we instruct Linkerd to use the
# existing certificate by setting the identity.issuer.scheme to
# kubernetes.io/tls.
$ helm install linkerd-control-plane -n linkerd \
  --set-file identityTrustAnchorsPEM=ca.crt \
  --set identity.issuer.scheme=kubernetes.io/tls \
  --version 1.12.4 \
  linkerd/linkerd-control-plane

# Validate the Linkerd install.
$ linkerd check

# You'll see warnings letting you know your Linkerd issuer certificate isn't
# valid for more than 60 days. That's to be expected, as you are now actively
# rotating the issuer certificate with cert-manager.
```

With that, you now have a fully functional Linkerd instance with an actively and automatically rotating issuer certificate. You've added a significant amount of security to your environment and ensured that your cluster will get new certificates on a regular basis. It's important to actively monitor cert-manager and check that your certificates are being rotated regularly. An expired issuer certificate is one of the few ways Linkerd can actively take down your applications, and its health and safety is critical to your platform.

Summary

We've covered a lot of ground in this chapter. mTLS and certificate handling are complex topics, even though they've been around for a long time. The challenge is that to properly secure a cloud native application, right now you need to know more about this stuff than you might like.

One of the ways that Linkerd simplifies the process of hardening your environment is making mTLS effectively automatic, allowing any Linkerd user to rely on mTLS's well-trusted identity and encryption mechanisms for secure communications. Another way is that Linkerd gives you control over critical certificate management operations: Linkerd's ability to issue certificates for your application's workloads, then rotate them frequently and automatically, gives you some powerful tools you need to reduce the likelihood and impact of any security incident.

# CHAPTER 8

Linkerd Policy: Overview and Server-Based Policy

Microservices applications, as we discussed in Chapter 7, require a different level of network security than more traditional monoliths. mTLS gives you the secure communications and workload identity that you need to start tackling this level of network security—but it's Linkerd's *policy* mechanisms that provide the ability to use that identity to control how workloads can talk to each other in your environment.

Linkerd supports two kinds of policy mechanisms: *Server-based* and *route-based*. Since policy is the single most complex area of Linkerd, we'll provide an overview and cover Server-based policy in this chapter, then tackle route-based policy in Chapter 9.

Linkerd Policy Overview

All Linkerd policy mechanisms are based on *explicit authorization*: Linkerd starts out assuming that it should allow nothing and must be explicitly told what requests should be allowed. This lines up nicely with the zero trust model and makes it straightforward to reason about permissions, since policy resources are always *permitting* things to happen.

Don't panic, though; this doesn't mean a policy is always a morass of hundreds of resources. Linkerd allows setting a *default policy* at the cluster, namespace, and Pod levels, with policy settings at more specific levels overriding policy settings at more general levels: Pods override namespaces, which override cluster-wide settings, as shown in Figure 8-1.

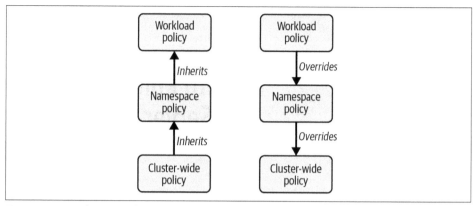

Figure 8-1. Different Linkerd default policy settings

It may seem strange to talk about defaults overriding defaults. Here, "default" is in contrast to the other kind of policy setting that Linkerd supports: using *dynamic policy resources*. The default policy is simply the policy that applies when no dynamic resource is present for a given request.

Policy is always enforced along Pod boundaries, since the Pod is the basic unit managed by Linkerd. It's not possible, for example, to write a policy that will affect communications with a single container in a Pod.

Linkerd Default Policy

Linkerd has the following default policy options:

all-unauthenticated
  Allow all traffic, whether authenticated or not.

cluster-unauthenticated
  Allow all traffic from *this cluster*.

all-authenticated
  Allow traffic from all meshed clients.

cluster-authenticated
  Allow traffic from meshed clients in *this cluster*.

deny
  Deny everything.

The distinction between all and cluster is relevant only if you're using multicluster (as discussed in Chapter 12). In a multicluster setting, all includes clients from other clusters, whereas cluster does not, as shown in Figure 8-2. If you're not using multicluster, the two are equivalent.

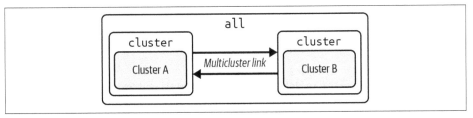

Figure 8-2. all versus cluster

The cluster default policy is set at install time with the proxy.defaultInboundPolicy value, as shown in Example 8-1. If not set, the cluster default policy will be all-unauthenticated: this allows absolutely any request, mirroring Kubernetes's default wide-open stance. Linkerd uses this default to ensure that users who don't want or need to use policy (or who just haven't gotten to that point in hardening their clusters yet) won't be negatively impacted when they install Linkerd.

Why the Permissive Default Policy?

Linkerd's default all-unauthenticated is obviously not good for security, and we *strongly* advise you to pick a different cluster default for production installations.

However, as a practical matter, literally any other base default almost guarantees that installing Linkerd into a running application would break things. Ultimately, all-unauthenticated as the base default is the only way to allow Linkerd to do no harm when first brought into an application, and that's *why* it's the base default.

Example 8-1. Setting the cluster default policy

```
# We can set the cluster's default policy with Helm...
$ helm install linkerd-control-plane -n linkerd \
    ... \
    --set proxy.defaultInboundPolicy=all-authenticated \
    ...

# ...or with the Linkerd CLI.
$ linkerd install \
      ...
      --set proxy.defaultInboundPolicy=all-authenticated \
      ... \
    | kubectl install -
```

To override the default for a namespace, workload, or Pod, you'll use the `config.linkerd.io/default-inbound-policy` annotation, setting it to one of the values listed earlier, as shown here:

```
$ kubectl annotate namespace your-namespace \
        config.linkerd.io/default-inbound-policy=all-authenticated
```

Linkerd Policy Resources

To override the default policy, you use policy resources, which are CRDs that configure which requests should be permitted:

Server
: Describes one or more Pods and one port on those Pods

HTTPRoute
: Describes a subset of the HTTP traffic to a given Server

MeshTLSAuthentication
: Describes one or more mesh identities

NetworkAuthentication
: Describes one or more IP addresses

AuthorizationPolicy
: Binds a Server or HTTPRoute to mesh or network authentications

These resources work together as shown in Figure 8-3; for example, an AuthorizationPolicy can link a Server and a MeshTLSAuthentication to permit a specific set of mesh identities to access the Server.

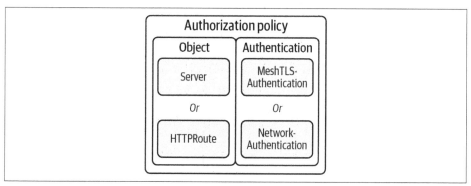

Figure 8-3. Linkerd policy resources

Let's take a closer look at each of these resources and how they're used to configure Linkerd policy.

Server

We talked about the Server resource briefly in Chapter 4. Server resources are specific to Linkerd; they allow describing a single specific port of a workload. For example, the Server in Example 8-2 describes the `http` port of the `foo` workload, which is the set of Pods with the `app: foo` label. This Server also notes that that port carries HTTP/1.1 traffic.

Example 8-2. A Server resource

```
apiVersion: policy.linkerd.io/v1beta1
kind: Server
metadata:
  name: foo
  namespace: foo-ns
spec:
  podSelector:
    matchLabels:
      app: foo
  port: http
  proxyProtocol: HTTP/1
```

Note that Server is a namespaced resource that must appear in the same namespace as the Pods it needs to match.

HTTPRoute

HTTPRoute is a Gateway API resource that describes specific HTTP requests. We'll discuss HTTPRoute more in Chapter 9.

MeshTLSAuthentication

MeshTLSAuthentication describes a particular set of mesh identities. Any workload running with one of the listed identities will match the MeshTLSAuthentication. For example, Example 8-3 shows a MeshTLSAuthentication for the single identity `foo.foo-ns.serviceaccount.identity.linkerd.cluster.local`.

Example 8-3. A MeshTLSAuthentication resource

```
apiVersion: policy.linkerd.io/v1alpha1
kind: MeshTLSAuthentication
metadata:
  name: foo
  namespace: foo-ns
spec:
  identities:
    - "foo.foo-ns.serviceaccount.identity.linkerd.cluster.local"
```

MeshTLSAuthentication is a namespaced resource. It will typically be placed in the same namespace as the workloads it's associated with, although this isn't a strict requirement.

NetworkAuthentication

A NetworkAuthentication resource describes a set of IP address CIDR ranges. Any request coming from one of the listed ranges will match the NetworkAuthentication.

Given that Linkerd makes such a big deal about using workload identity rather than network identity, it may seem strange that the NetworkAuthentication resource exists at all; however, as a practical matter, it can be useful at times when managing unmeshed clients.

NetworkAuthentication is a namespaced resource. It will typically be placed in the same namespace as the workloads it's associated with, although this isn't a strict requirement.

AuthorizationPolicy

Linkerd AuthorizationPolicy resources *permit access* to a *target* for some *required authentications*. The target, at present, must be a Server or an HTTPRoute. The required authentications must be one or more MeshTLSAuthentication or Network Authentication resources.

AuthorizationPolicy is a namespaced resource. It will typically be placed in the same namespace as the workloads it's associated with, although this isn't a strict requirement.

We'll go deeper into the individual objects as we begin actually using policy to lock down our cluster.

Server-Based Policy Versus Route-Based Policy

Server-based policy gets its name because it relies on Linkerd Server resources. You'll note that while the Server resource describes a workload and port, it does *not* describe anything about requests. This means that Server-based policy can't differentiate separate requests to a given Server, instead requiring every request going to a Server to adhere to the same policy.

Route-based policy (which we'll discuss in Chapter 9), on the other hand, *does* get to take request details into account. It is a more powerful—and also more complex—mechanism.

Server-Based Policy with the emojivoto Application

We'll use the emojivoto sample application (*https://oreil.ly/g7fDb*) to illustrate work-ing with policy in Linkerd. For reference, Figure 8-4 shows our end goal: the entire emojivoto application will be protected from accesses that shouldn't happen.

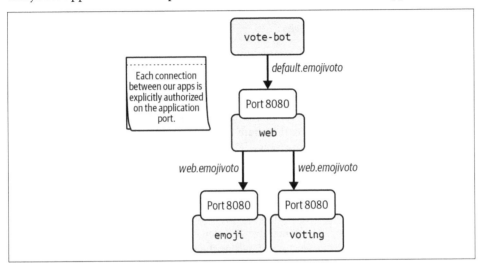

Figure 8-4. emojivoto policy overview

In this chapter, we'll guide you through a few different patterns you can adopt for your cluster, each of which will progressively lock down your applications and what they can communicate with.

Configuring the Default Policy

The first step we can take to lock down our clusters is also one of the most impactful and wide-ranging. Linkerd provides a straightforward mechanism for setting the default inbound policy for all of our proxies. In this section we're going to show you how to set the default inbound policy at the cluster and namespace level.

Cluster default policy

Let's start by setting the default policy for the entire cluster. Remember, when you install Linkerd, the default policy for the whole cluster is all-unauthenticated, which allows absolutely any request, mirroring Kubernetes's default wide-open stance.

We'll start by switching the default policy for the cluster to all-authenticated. This will require that all connections to meshed Pods come from other Pods that are in the mesh. This is good for security, but adds some operational overhead since you'll need to carve out exceptions for any nonmeshed applications that you want to continue being able to talk to meshed Pods. For example, imagine that you have a nonmeshed monitoring tool: when you flip the default to `all-authenticated`, it will suddenly be unable to talk to your meshed Pods, and you'll either need to mesh the monitoring tool or add an exception to your Linkerd policy for it.

To Deny or Not to Deny

In a perfect world, your entire cluster would have its default policy set to deny. This is absolutely the best practice from a security perspective, but if you're starting with an existing application, adding Linkerd with the default set to deny is very likely to break things unless you know *all* of the different traffic that you'll need to permit. In practice, that's rare if you weren't already working with fine-grained security tools.

An effective and practical compromise can be to start with `all-unauthenticated`, then use Linkerd's observability tools to determine what traffic should be permitted before gradually tightening security via `all-authenticated` or `cluster-authenticated` on the way to deny. Also remember that you can switch specific namespaces to deny as steps toward getting the whole cluster to deny.

In a *nonproduction* environment, of course, the broad stroke of just flipping everything to deny and watching what breaks is a *great* way to see exactly what communications are happening that you haven't thought of yet. Just don't go there in production!

Because the cluster-wide policy is a global setting, we'll configure it using Helm. In Example 8-4, we'll use `helm upgrade` to change Linkerd's settings without changing the version of Linkerd you have installed. This example assumes you're using Linkerd 2.13.4.

Example 8-4. Cluster policy

```
# Use helm upgrade to set the global inbound policy to all-authenticated.
$ helm upgrade linkerd-control-plane -n linkerd \
  --set proxy.defaultInboundPolicy=all-authenticated \
  --version  1.12.4 \
  --reuse-values \
  linkerd/linkerd-control-plane

# Now we can install the emojivoto app in our cluster to validate that it
# can operate normally while meshed.
$ curl --proto '=https' --tlsv1.2 -sSfL https://run.linkerd.io/emojivoto.yml \
  | linkerd inject - | kubectl apply -f -
```

```
# Once your Pods are up and running, test the emojivoto application to see
# if it's still working.
$ kubectl -n emojivoto port-forward svc/web-svc 8080:80

# Now browse to localhost:8080 and look at the emojivoto app. You should
# see the normal voting page.
```

Namespace default policy

Going further, we can flip the emojivoto namespace to deny to further protect our application, as shown in Example 8-5. Once we do this, *all* traffic in the namespace will be denied unless we explicitly authorize it.

Example 8-5. Namespace policy

```
# Start by using kubectl to annotate the namespace. We're going to set it
# to deny all traffic that hasn't been explicitly authorized.
$ kubectl annotate namespace emojivoto config.linkerd.io/default-inbound-policy=deny

# With that done, the policy changes won't have any impact on the Pods that
# are already running. You will need to perform a rollout restart for the
# new default policy to take effect.
$ kubectl rollout restart deploy -n emojivoto

# Once your Pods are up and running, test the emojivoto application to see
# if it's still working.
$ kubectl -n emojivoto port-forward svc/web-svc 8080:80

# Now browse to localhost:8080 and look at the emojivoto app. You should now
# see the page load, but all the emojis are gone. That is because the web
# frontend can no longer talk to either of its backends, voting or emoji.
```

Timing Matters

Linkerd's default inbound policy is read by your proxies at startup time. It is not read dynamically. This is important for operators to be aware of because it means any changes you make only take effect when your Pods are created. If you change the default inbound policy for the cluster or a namespace, those changes will only take effect after the Pods in your namespace are re-created. Pod-level inbound policy changes will take effect when the Kubernetes API restarts the modified Pods, so they will effectively get applied as soon as you modify the Deployments, StatefulSets, or DaemonSets in question.

With that, we've managed to block communication between our workloads in the emojivoto namespace…and *everything* is broken. To make the app work again, we need to start allowing necessary traffic again with *dynamic policy*.

Configuring Dynamic Policy

As demonstrated, it's not very useful just to use defaults to block everything. It's time to look at how to use our dynamic policy resources to allow useful, necessary traffic to flow. We'll start with a fairly simple concept: many organizations treat namespaces as logical boundaries between applications or teams, so it often makes sense to allow workloads in the same namespace to talk to each other. This is commonly called *namespace isolation*.

Namespace isolation

With namespace isolation, we can easily restrict traffic in a namespace exclusively to those workloads that share that namespace. In our example, we'll start by permitting traffic within the emojivoto namespace as long as the source and destination identities are *both* within this single namespace. This makes sense for the emojivoto application because the only things running in its namespace are parts of emojivoto itself: it's a natural result of the idea that the application is contained within a single namespace.

Identities, Not IP Addresses

Note that we said "source and destination *identities*." Everything Linkerd does with policy is based on the workload identity, not the workload's IP address or anything else about the network. The workloads don't even need to be in the same cluster, as long as the identities line up.

We'll set up namespace isolation for emojivoto in Example 8-6. Fair warning: this will look complex. The inline comments are very important to fully understand exactly what's going on in this example.

Example 8-6. Namespace isolation for emojivoto

```
# To start applying policies to the emojivoto workloads, we need to create
# Server objects. A Server object selects a single named port on one or more
# Pods.
#
# We'll start by setting up a Server that matches the Linkerd admin port,
# used for metrics, for every Pod in our namespace.
$ kubectl apply -f - <<EOF
apiVersion: policy.linkerd.io/v1beta1
kind: Server
metadata:
  namespace: emojivoto
  name: linkerd-admin
spec:
  podSelector:
    matchLabels: {}
  port: linkerd-admin
  proxyProtocol: HTTP/2
EOF

# This object, a Server called linkerd, will, due to our matchLabels selector,
# match every Pod in our namespace. On each Pod it will bind to a port named
# linkerd-admin and allow us to apply policy to it.
#
# Next, we will create a Server object for each part of our application,
# starting with the web service (which serves the GUI).
$ kubectl apply -f - <<EOF
apiVersion: policy.linkerd.io/v1beta1
kind: Server
metadata:
  namespace: emojivoto
  name: web-http
  labels:
    app.kubernetes.io/part-of: emojivoto
    app.kubernetes.io/name: web
    app.kubernetes.io/version: v11
spec:
  podSelector:
    matchLabels:
      app: web-svc
  port: http
  proxyProtocol: HTTP/1
EOF
```

```
# The Server web-http matches the HTTP port for Pods that are part of the
# web service by selecting any Pods with the app=web-svc label. It also has
# the added benefit of allowing us to skip protocol detection on this port
# by specifying the protocol as HTTP/1.
#
# Now we'll create the Servers for emojivoto's backing services,
# voting and emoji.
$ kubectl apply -f - <<EOF
---
apiVersion: policy.linkerd.io/v1beta1
kind: Server
metadata:
  namespace: emojivoto
  name: emoji-grpc
  labels:
    app.kubernetes.io/part-of: emojivoto
    app.kubernetes.io/name: emoji
    app.kubernetes.io/version: v11
    app: emoji-svc
    emojivoto/api: internal-grpc
spec:
  podSelector:
    matchLabels:
      app: emoji-svc
  port: grpc
  proxyProtocol: gRPC
---
apiVersion: policy.linkerd.io/v1beta1
kind: Server
metadata:
  namespace: emojivoto
  name: voting-grpc
  labels:
    app: voting-svc
    emojivoto/api: internal-grpc
spec:
  podSelector:
    matchLabels:
      app: voting-svc
  port: grpc
  proxyProtocol: gRPC
EOF
```

```
# These are basically the same idea as the web Server, just with different
# label selectors. Also, since emojivoto uses gRPC for these workloads, we
# set the protocol to gRPC.
#
# With that, all of our Servers have been created, and we are ready to begin
# to allow communication within our namespace. We'll next define a single
# MeshTLSAuthentication resource that matches all service accounts within
# the emojivoto namespace.
$ kubectl apply -f - <<EOF
apiVersion: policy.linkerd.io/v1alpha1
kind: MeshTLSAuthentication
metadata:
  name: emojivoto-accounts
  namespace: emojivoto
spec:
  identities:
    - "*.emojivoto.serviceaccount.identity.linkerd.cluster.local"
EOF

# Then, we will bind that MeshTLSAuthentication to our Servers. We could do it
# individually on a port-by-port basis, but in this case it's simpler to bind
# to every policy object in the namespace.
$ kubectl apply -f - <<EOF
apiVersion: policy.linkerd.io/v1alpha1
kind: AuthorizationPolicy
metadata:
  name: emojivoto-only
  namespace: emojivoto
  labels:
    app.kubernetes.io/part-of: emojivoto
    project: emojivoto
spec:
  targetRef:
    kind: Namespace
    name: emojivoto
  requiredAuthenticationRefs:
    - name: emojivoto-accounts
      kind: MeshTLSAuthentication
      group: policy.linkerd.io
EOF

# With that, we should see that the emojivoto workloads are able to communicate
# with each other once again. You can check this by using a port forward to
# look at the emojivoto app's GUI: start this forwarder, then open
# http://localhost:8080/ in your browser.
$ kubectl -n emojivoto port-forward svc/web-svc 8080:80
```

What's in a Name?

Linkerd Server objects are the core construct that allows us to apply policy to our applications. They work by matching Pods based on some selection criteria and then selecting a port *by the port's name*. Kubernetes will allow you to create Pods without adding a name to a port, so you must be sure that when using Linkerd policy in your cluster, every port in your applications has a value set for its name.

We know that was a lot of YAML! Policy definition is the most labor-intensive task you'll need to undertake to use Linkerd. Luckily for all of us, policy is an opt-in feature that you can prepare for in advance of turning it on. We *strongly* recommend you thoroughly test all your policy objects in a nonproduction environment before applying them to a live environment.

Test Early, Test Often

This bears repeating. *Policy is complex* and easy to get wrong. We *strongly* encourage that you test your policy definitions in a nonproduction environment before taking them to production.

Allowing Linkerd Viz

At this point, we've isolated the emojivoto namespace within the cluster: nothing from outside the namespace gets to speak with anything inside the namespace. Unfortunately, this will break things like monitoring applications and ingress controllers. This is decidedly less than ideal: while we've done a lot to secure our emojivoto namespace, we've caused other problems. For example, we've left any potential operations folks with little to no ability to monitor what our emojivoto workloads are doing.

To fix this, we can use dynamic policy resources that reference identities from *outside* the namespace. In Example 8-7 we'll walk you through installing Linkerd Viz and allowing it to poll your applications, as shown in Figure 8-5.

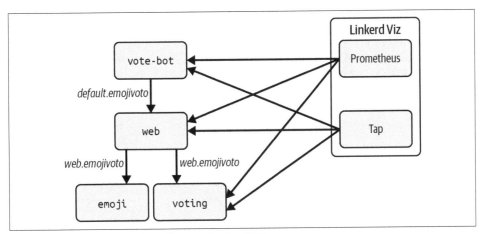

Figure 8-5. emojivoto policy allowing Linkerd Viz

Example 8-7. Let there be Viz!

```
# Let's install the Linkerd Viz extension. We'll continue our theme of
# installing things with Helm.
$ helm install linkerd-viz linkerd/linkerd-viz \
  -n linkerd-viz \
  --create-namespace \
  --version 30.8.4

# This command will install the linkerd 2.13.4 version of Linkerd's Viz
# extension.
#
# Once that's done, wait for Viz to be ready.
$ linkerd check

# We now want to restart our emojivoto workloads so that they start
# collecting Tap data. This is critical for observability.
$ kubectl rollout restart deploy -n emojivoto

# With that complete, we can now move on to validating that the Linkerd
# Viz extension is unable to talk to our workloads.
$ linkerd viz stat deploy -n emojivoto

# You should see all your deployments with no statistics associated with
# them. That's because Linkerd's Prometheus instance is located in the
# linkerd-viz namespace, and it hasn't been given permission to talk to
# anything in the emojivoto namespace.
```

```
# Let's fix that now. First, we define a MeshTLSAuthentication resource
# that matches the identities used by Tap and Prometheus, which are the
# parts of Linkerd Viz that collect data.
$ kubectl apply -f - <<EOF
apiVersion: policy.linkerd.io/v1alpha1
kind: MeshTLSAuthentication
metadata:
  name: linkerd-viz
  namespace: emojivoto
spec:
  identities:
    - "tap.linkerd-viz.serviceaccount.identity.linkerd.cluster.local"
    - "prometheus.linkerd-viz.serviceaccount.identity.linkerd.cluster.local"
EOF

# Next, we permit that MeshTLSAuthentication to talk to Pods in the
# emojivoto namespace, using an AuthorizationPolicy as before.
$ kubectl apply -f - <<EOF
apiVersion: policy.linkerd.io/v1alpha1
kind: AuthorizationPolicy
metadata:
  name: allow-viz
  namespace: emojivoto
spec:
  targetRef:
    kind: Namespace
    name: emojivoto
  requiredAuthenticationRefs:
    - name: linkerd-viz
      kind: MeshTLSAuthentication
      group: policy.linkerd.io
EOF

# At this point, Tap and Prometheus should be happily collecting data.
# Give them a minute or so to get something substantive, then you should
# be able to see good results from a second "linkerd viz stat" command.
$ linkerd viz stat deploy -n emojivoto
```

With that complete, we've now walked through what you need to do to isolate traffic within a namespace but still allow in an external monitoring tool like the Linkerd Viz extension. You now have the basic knowledge required to begin isolating your own workloads by namespace with Linkerd's policy tools. Next, we'll get a little more granular and only allow specific service accounts to access our workloads.

Locking down by port and identity

Namespace isolation goes a long way to further hardening our environment, but we can go further than that. With the isolation we've applied so far, any request is allowed as long as the calling workload and the called workload are both in the emoji voto namespace, but this is probably more permissive than we really need. To go a little further, we can be explicit about which accounts are allowed to talk to which workloads—but of course, that requires knowing exactly which communications are truly required by the application.

Figuring out those requirements by inspecting code is tedious and error-prone, but fortunately we can do better than that by using tools like Linkerd Viz (or its commercial cousins from Buoyant) to help us map our application's communication and build our policy objects.

We need only a single Linkerd Viz CLI command to see which workloads are communicating with one another in the emojivoto namespace:

```
$ linkerd viz edges deploy -n emojivoto
```

This will produce a list of Deployments that are communicating with one another in this namespace. Deployments listed under the SRC column are the sources (clients) for requests; those listed under DST are the destinations (servers).

If you'd prefer to investigate using the Viz dashboard rather than its CLI, you can run:

```
$ linkerd viz dashboard
```

The Viz dashboard is out of scope for this book, but it's fairly intuitive, and we encourage you to poke around in it if you haven't had the chance to use it before.

From the output we can see the connections between our emojivoto workloads, as shown in Figure 8-6.

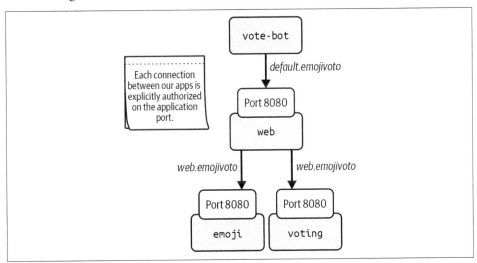

Figure 8-6. emojivoto inter-workload communications

emojivoto is a very simple application, so there are only three connections:

- vote-bot talks to the web Deployment.
- web communicates with voting.
- web communicates with emoji.

With that, we can begin building policy. We'll start by gathering the Subject names on our individual workloads, as shown in Example 8-8. We'll need to gather the names for vote-bot and web. We don't need to allow voting or emoji to communicate with any other services, as neither of them act as clients for any other services.

Example 8-8. Gathering Subject names

```
# Start by grabbing the name of the first vote-bot Pod (which should
# be the only vote-bot Pod).
#
# This kubectl command uses -l app=vote-bot to pick all Pods with the
# "app: vote-bot" label, then uses JSONPath to pick the metadata.name
# of the first Pod in the list.
$ VOTEBOTPOD=$(kubectl get pods -n emojivoto -l app=vote-bot \
            -o jsonpath='{ .items[0].metadata.name }')

# Now use the Pod name for vote-bot to get the Subject name.
$ linkerd identity $VOTEBOTPOD -n emojivoto | grep Subject:

# This will print out the Subject name for the vote-bot Pod, which is
# the name of that Pod's identity. It will look like:
#
#   Subject: CN=default.emojivoto.serviceaccount.identity.linkerd.cluster.local
#
# We only want the part after CN=, so
# default.emojivoto.serviceaccount.identity.linkerd.cluster.local.

# Repeat for the web Pod, which we can find using the "app: web-svc" label.
$ WEBPOD=$(kubectl get pods -n emojivoto -l app=web-svc \
          -o jsonpath='{ .items[0].metadata.name }')

$ linkerd identity $WEBPOD -n emojivoto | grep Subject:

# It should output a name like:
#   Subject: CN=web.emojivoto.serviceaccount.identity.linkerd.cluster.local
#
# and again, we'll want the part after CN=:
# web.emojivoto.serviceaccount.identity.linkerd.cluster.local
```

What's in a Name?

Why does the `vote-bot` workload get an identity named "default" while the `web` workload gets one named "web"? If you look carefully at the `vote-bot` and `web` Deployments, you'll find that `web` specifies which ServiceAccount to use, but `vote-bot` does not...so `vote-bot` gets the default. *This is not a best practice*. In a perfect world, every workload would get its own ServiceAccount.

We're showing this because while it's not ideal, it's *very* common to see this default ServiceAccount in use when trying to set up policy for applications that weren't designed with zero trust in mind—and you may need to create new ServiceAccounts in addition to creating policy resources!

With those two Subject names, we can update our policy to be much more explicit about who is allowed to talk to whom in the `emojivoto` namespace. It's worth remembering that in the previous section we created a number of policy objects that allow the emojivoto workloads to talk to each other. In Example 8-9, we'll be reusing some and removing others in order to move from a more permissive to less permissive security posture, as shown in Figure 8-7.

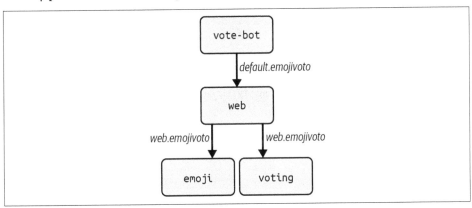

Figure 8-7. emojivoto less permissive model

Server-Side Policy

In Linkerd, the workload-based policy engine enforces all policy decisions on the server side. When we configure deny as the default in our environment, we have to go through each server individually to ensure all its clients have been explicitly allowed.

Example 8-9. Restricting interapp communication

```
# We'll start by creating two new MeshTLSAuthentication objects. The
# first allows only the default identity (currently used by the vote-bot);
# the second allows only the web identity.
$ kubectl apply -f - <<EOF
apiVersion: policy.linkerd.io/v1alpha1
kind: MeshTLSAuthentication
metadata:
  name: default
  namespace: emojivoto
spec:
  identities:
  - 'default.emojivoto.serviceaccount.identity.linkerd.cluster.local'
---
apiVersion: policy.linkerd.io/v1alpha1
kind: MeshTLSAuthentication
metadata:
  name: web
  namespace: emojivoto
spec:
  identities:
  - 'web.emojivoto.serviceaccount.identity.linkerd.cluster.local'
EOF
```

```
# Each object corresponds to either the vote-bot or web application. We
# inserted the names we gathered in Example 8-8 to populate these
# objects. It's a good practice to name them after the identity they
# represent, rather than the workload -- in particular, the "default"
# identity is probably used by more than just the vote-bot, so we don't
# want to name that MeshTLSAuthentication "vote-bot" as that might give
# the impression that we need only think about the vote-bot when using
# that!

# With that done, we can begin binding those authentications to our servers.
# We'll start with allowing vote-bot (using the default identity) to talk
# to web.
$ kubectl apply -f - <<EOF
apiVersion: policy.linkerd.io/v1alpha1
kind: AuthorizationPolicy
metadata:
  labels:
    app.kubernetes.io/part-of: emojivoto
    project: emojivoto
  name: allow-default-to-web
  namespace: emojivoto
spec:
  requiredAuthenticationRefs:
  - group: policy.linkerd.io
    kind: MeshTLSAuthentication
    name: default
  targetRef:
    group: policy.linkerd.io
    kind: Server
    name: web-http
EOF
```

```
# This AuthorizationPolicy will allow any workload using the default
# identity to talk to the web workload, using the "web-http" Server we
# already created.

# Now we will give the web application access to emoji and voting. In
# order to accomplish this we will need to create two AuthorizationPolicy
# objects, one for each Server.
$ kubectl apply -f - <<EOF
apiVersion: policy.linkerd.io/v1alpha1
kind: AuthorizationPolicy
metadata:
  labels:
    app.kubernetes.io/part-of: emojivoto
    project: emojivoto
  name: allow-web-to-voting
  namespace: emojivoto
spec:
  requiredAuthenticationRefs:
  - group: policy.linkerd.io
    kind: MeshTLSAuthentication
    name: web
  targetRef:
    group: policy.linkerd.io
    kind: Server
    name: voting-grpc
---
apiVersion: policy.linkerd.io/v1alpha1
kind: AuthorizationPolicy
metadata:
  labels:
    app.kubernetes.io/part-of: emojivoto
    project: emojivoto
  name: allow-web-to-emoji
  namespace: emojivoto
spec:
  requiredAuthenticationRefs:
  - group: policy.linkerd.io
    kind: MeshTLSAuthentication
    name: web
  targetRef:
    group: policy.linkerd.io
    kind: Server
    name: emoji-grpc
EOF
```

```
# Here, the allow-web-to-voting AuthorizationPolicy allows any workload
# using the web identity to talk to the voting workload; allow-web-to-emoji
# does the same for the emoji workload. Again, we're using Servers we created
# earlier.

# Now that we have our new policies in place, we can delete the policies that
# allow all the apps in the emojivoto namespace to talk to one another.
$ kubectl delete authorizationpolicies.policy.linkerd.io emojivoto-only -n emojivoto

# Finally, we'll use a port forward to test the emojivoto app and be sure it
# still operates normally.
$ kubectl -n emojivoto port-forward svc/web-svc 8080:80
```

Order of Operations

As we moved from namespace-wide permissions to more specific permissions, we created our new policy objects before removing the namespace-wide permissions. If we had inverted the order, we would have disrupted communication between the emojivoto workloads.

You have now further restricted access to the apps in the emojivoto namespace. Now communication between your workloads will occur only if it has been explicitly authorized by your platform team. Every denial is logged by the Linkerd proxy, and your security team can use these logs to identify malicious behavior in your clusters. Hopefully you can see how this sort of hardening dramatically reduces the risk of an intrusion in your environment and, with proper monitoring and logging, dramatically increases the likelihood that suspicious behavior will be caught.

Summary

Linkerd's Server-based policy is its oldest policy mechanism, but it's still incredibly effective in a great many situations. Server-based policy gives you the ability to set known, trustworthy defaults while also making it straightforward to tune everything for your application, and Linkerd's Tap ability lets you quickly get a sense of what you need to sort out.

# CHAPTER 9

Linkerd Route-Based Policy

In Chapter 8, we discussed implementing a Linkerd Server-based policy to enhance the security of the emojivoto application. This policy ensures that Linkerd effectively safeguards the application's workload, preventing unauthorized workloads from making requests. Suppose we want to go further, though? For example, consider a situation where you have a sensitive application. You need to be certain that only specific ServiceAccounts are allowed to make changes, and only certain others have access to read.

That's where Linkerd's route-based policy mechanism comes in. In this chapter, we'll take a closer look at what route-based policy can do and how to use it.

Route-Based Policy Overview

Route-based policy gives Linkerd a way to express policy that depends not only on which workloads are in play, but also on which specific requests are being made. These specific HTTP requests are identified by using Gateway API HTTPRoute resources to specify matches against the HTTP path, method, headers, etc.—almost anything except the body can be used. Requests are still authenticated using mTLS identities.

Gateway API HTTPRoute resources work by associating one or more *parents* with one or more *rules*. When using Gateway API for ingress, the parents of an HTTPRoute will be Gateway resources; however, this doesn't make much sense when using Gateway API to configure a service mesh. When using HTTPRoutes with Linkerd, the parents will be Services instead, and the HTTPRoute will only apply to traffic that is directed to the parent Service *and* that matches a rule specified by the HTTPRoute.

HTTPRoutes, Gateway API, and You

Linkerd 2.13 supports the HTTPRoute object, but it actually uses a copy in the `policy.linkerd.io/v1` API group, rather than the official `gateway.networking.k8s.io/v1beta1` HTTPRoute. This sidesteps issues around Gateway API conformance.

When Linkerd 2.13 shipped, it wasn't possible for a service mesh to be conformant to the Gateway API standard. By Linkerd 2.14, Gateway API had defined the `Mesh` *conformance profile*, which specifies what it means for a service mesh to be conformant with Gateway API. Linkerd 2.14 and higher are conformant with the `Mesh` profile and support the `gateway.networking.k8s.io/v1beta1` HTTPRoute (as well as the older copy that Linkerd 2.13 supported). The end result is that some tools that rely on the HTTPRoute object aren't fully compatible with Linkerd 2.13, but they're happier with Linkerd 2.14 and higher.

(If you want to know more about all of this stuff, check out the Gateway API introduction (*https://oreil.ly/n0mtd*) and read about Gateway API and the GAMMA initiative.)

Route-based policy is the most detailed and granular level of policy in Linkerd, and using it requires a significant amount of planning and a significant amount of YAML. When you're ready to secure your environments to this degree, you need to be aware of the cost in terms of engineering time and effort. We also *strongly* recommend that when building any kind of policy you use multiple environments—at least one for building and testing policy, and another for enforcing it. Ideally, you'll integrate policy creation, auditing, and promotion into your standard application development lifecycle.

The booksapp Sample Application

We'll be using the booksapp sample application (*https://oreil.ly/qf8il*) to show how you can use route-based policy to restrict calls based not just on the workload, but also on the specific endpoints being accessed.

As shown in Figure 9-1, the app is very similar to emojivoto.

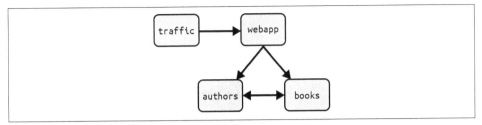

Figure 9-1. booksapp interapplication connections

In booksapp, two of our backing services (`books` and `authors`) need to talk to each other—but they shouldn't all have unrestricted access to each other. For example, the `authors` workload should have access to read from the `books` workload, so that it can show the books each author has written. The UI for `authors` also allows you to add a new book for the author you're looking at, so `authors` needs to be able to POST new books to `books`. However, it mustn't be able to modify or delete books.

Ultimately, we want to allow only the following requests, and no others:

- Infrastructure:
  - The `kubelet` needs to be able to run health checks for all our workloads.
  - Linkerd Viz needs to be able to scrape metrics from all workloads.
- Core application functionality:
  - `webapp` needs to be able to read, create, delete, and update both `authors` and `books`.
  - `authors` needs to be able to read and create `books`.
  - `books` needs to be able to read and create `authors`.
- Traffic generator:
  - `traffic` needs to have full access to `webapp`.

This can be seen in Figure 9-2.

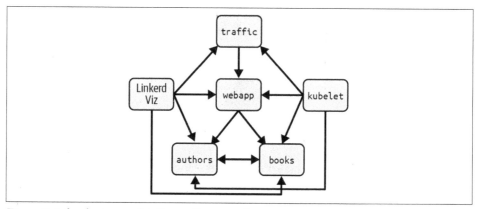

Figure 9-2. booksapp application policy overview

Installing booksapp

The setup is fairly simple. We'll pull down the latest version of the booksapp application, add the Linkerd proxy, and apply it to our cluster, as shown in Example 9-1.

Example 9-1. Setup

```
# Install booksapp...
$ kubectl create ns booksapp && \
  curl --proto '=https' --tlsv1.2 -sSfL https://run.linkerd.io/booksapp.yml \
  | linkerd inject - \
  | kubectl -n booksapp apply -f -

# Wait for Pods to be running...
$ kubectl rollout status -n booksapp deploy

# ...then test using a port forward.
$ kubectl -n booksapp port-forward svc/webapp 8080:80

# Now browse to localhost:8080.
```

Configuring booksapp Policy

At this point, booksapp is running with no restrictions: everything can access everything else. This is often the simplest place to start when working with policy; once you know that the application is working, you can start tightening things up.

We'll work through our booksapp policy in steps:

1. At the start, we'll work on the low-level infrastructure, switching to default deny and allowing Linkerd Viz to still work. We'll use Server-based policy for this; it doesn't require the granularity of route-based policy, so we'll avoid the complexity.

2. We'll next configure minimal route-based policy to allow read-only access to the application.

3. We'll then allow writes to the authors workload, then the books workload.

4. Finally, we'll allow access from the traffic generator to the webapp.

The advantage of doing things in this order is that it should quickly make it possible to see at least part of the application working, and we can do incremental testing. This is usually a very good idea when doing complex configuration, and (as we've said before) route-based policy is very complex.

Infrastructure Policy

The first step is infrastructure policy. We'll switch the booksapp namespace to default deny using a Server-based policy. In turn, this will require us to explicitly permit Linkerd Viz to keep working. All of this is shown in Example 9-2.

Example 9-2. books-infra-policy.yaml

```
# Create books-infra-policy.yaml.
$ cat <<EOF > books-infra-policy.yaml
---
apiVersion: policy.linkerd.io/v1beta1
kind: Server
metadata:
  namespace: booksapp
  name: linkerd-admin
spec:
  podSelector:
    matchLabels: {}
  port: linkerd-admin
  proxyProtocol: HTTP/2
---
apiVersion: policy.linkerd.io/v1alpha1
kind: AuthorizationPolicy
metadata:
  name: allow-viz
  namespace: booksapp
spec:
  targetRef:
    kind: Namespace
    name: booksapp
  requiredAuthenticationRefs:
    - name: linkerd-viz
      kind: MeshTLSAuthentication
      group: policy.linkerd.io
---
apiVersion: policy.linkerd.io/v1alpha1
kind: MeshTLSAuthentication
metadata:
  name: linkerd-viz
  namespace: booksapp
spec:
  identities:
    - "tap.linkerd-viz.serviceaccount.identity.linkerd.cluster.local"
    - "prometheus.linkerd-viz.serviceaccount.identity.linkerd.cluster.local"
EOF
```

This is similar to what we did in Chapter 8 to allow Linkerd Viz. Let's go ahead and apply the infrastructure policy YAML, then switch the booksapp namespace to default deny, as shown in Example 9-3.

Example 9-3. Setting up infrastructure policy

```
# Apply the YAML we just created...
$ kubectl apply -f books-infra-policy.yaml

# Switch `booksapp` to default deny...
$ kubectl annotate namespace booksapp config.linkerd.io/default-inbound-policy=deny

# ...and finally, restart the booksapp workloads.
$ kubectl rollout restart deployment -n booksapp
```

What About Health Checks?

The astute observer will notice that while our Pods have readiness and liveness probes configured, they're still starting and staying ready even though we haven't carved out any explicit authorizations for the kubelet to probe our Pods. That's because Linkerd will, by default, look for liveness and readiness probes for your applications and create a default HTTPRoute that will allow that traffic—but it will only do this *as long as you haven't created HTTPRoutes yourself.*

As soon as you begin creating your own HTTPRoutes for your application, Linkerd will delete its default routes, which means that you'll need to ensure that you create routes for your liveness and readiness probes.

At this point, with the booksapp namespace switched to default deny and only Viz authorized, our application won't work at all. Let's continue with getting our app running.

Read-Only Access

The next thing we'll do is use route-based policy to allow read-only access to the application. We'll be able to use a web browser to look up books and authors, but we won't be able to change anything.

Everything we're doing from this point forward is just applying YAML, so we'll just show the YAML that you need to apply. We'll do this from the inside out, so our first step is to permit the books workload to fetch /authors.json and /authors/ from the authors workload. This requires four resources.

First up, we need to define a Server for the authors workload in the books namespace, as shown in Example 9-4. This will allow us to use an HTTPRoute to configure policy for specific requests being made to the authors workload.

Example 9-4. authors Server

```
---
apiVersion: policy.linkerd.io/v1beta1
kind: Server
metadata:
  namespace: booksapp
  name: authors
  labels:
    app: authors
    app.kubernetes.io/part-of: booksapp
    project: booksapp
spec:
  podSelector:
    matchLabels:
      app: authors
      project: booksapp
  port: service
  proxyProtocol: HTTP/1
```

Next, we'll create an HTTPRoute specifying the two requests that we want to allow, as shown in Example 9-5.

Example 9-5. authors HTTPRoute

```
---
apiVersion: policy.linkerd.io/v1beta1
kind: HTTPRoute
metadata:
  name: authors-get-route
  namespace: booksapp
  labels:
    app.kubernetes.io/part-of: booksapp
    project: booksapp
spec:
  parentRefs:
    - name: authors
      kind: Server
      group: policy.linkerd.io
  rules:
    - matches:
      - path:
          value: "/authors.json"
        method: GET
      - path:
          value: "/authors/"
          type: "PathPrefix"
        method: GET
```

Which HTTPRoute?

We've used `policy.linkerd.io` HTTPRoutes to accommodate
readers with older versions of Linkerd. If you're using Linkerd
2.14 or newer, though, feel free to switch to `gateway.networking`
`.k8s.io/v1beta1` HTTPRoutes!

Finally, we can specify an AuthorizationPolicy/MeshTLSAuthentication pair, where
the `targetRef` of the AuthorizationPolicy is the HTTPRoute we just defined, to
define which identities are allowed to use this HTTPRoute, as shown in Example 9-6.

Example 9-6. authors AuthorizationPolicy and MeshTLSAuthentication

```
---
apiVersion: policy.linkerd.io/v1alpha1
kind: AuthorizationPolicy
metadata:
  name: allow-books-to-authors
  namespace: booksapp
  labels:
    app.kubernetes.io/part-of: booksapp
    project: booksapp
spec:
  targetRef:
    group: policy.linkerd.io
    kind: HTTPRoute
    name: authors-get-route
  requiredAuthenticationRefs:
    - name: books
      kind: MeshTLSAuthentication
      group: policy.linkerd.io
---
apiVersion: policy.linkerd.io/v1alpha1
kind: MeshTLSAuthentication
metadata:
  name: books
  namespace: booksapp
spec:
  identities:
    - "books.booksapp.serviceaccount.identity.linkerd.cluster.local"
```

Once these resources are applied, the `books` workload will be able to talk to the
`authors` workload. However, we've just broken health checks for the `authors` workload, as we noted earlier. As soon as we attached our HTTPRoute to the `authors`
Server, the probe routes generated by Linkerd went away.

To allow those probe requests, we'll use a separate HTTPRoute, which will allow
us to use a NetworkAuthorization to permit unauthenticated probe requests from
anywhere in our cluster. We definitely don't want to permit any other requests to

use that NetworkAuthorization, so we really do need a separate HTTPRoute for the probes! This is shown in Example 9-7.

Example 9-7. Re-permitting authors health probes

```
---
apiVersion: policy.linkerd.io/v1beta1
kind: HTTPRoute
metadata:
  name: books-probes
  namespace: booksapp
spec:
  parentRefs:
    - name: authors
      kind: Server
      group: policy.linkerd.io
  rules:
    - matches:
      - path:
          value: "/ping"
        method: GET
---
apiVersion: policy.linkerd.io/v1alpha1
kind: AuthorizationPolicy
metadata:
  name: authors-probe
  namespace: booksapp
spec:
  targetRef:
    group: policy.linkerd.io
    kind: HTTPRoute
    name: books-probes
  requiredAuthenticationRefs:
    - name: probe-authn
      kind: NetworkAuthentication
      group: policy.linkerd.io
---
apiVersion: policy.linkerd.io/v1alpha1
kind: NetworkAuthentication
metadata:
  name: probe-authn
  namespace: booksapp
spec:
  networks:
  - cidr: 0.0.0.0/0
  - cidr: ::/0
```

What's in a CIDR?

The `probe-authn` NetworkAuthorization is unnecessarily broad; it should really be limited just to the Pod CIDR range for your cluster. We can't predict that, so you should feel free to replace the CIDR ranges in the `probe-authn` NetworkAuthentication resource with the appropriate values for your cluster.

At this point, the `books` workload should be able to read from the `authors` workload, and probes to the `authors` workload should work as well. Now we need to repeat all of this to permit the `authors` workload to talk to `books`, as shown in Example 9-8.

Example 9-8. Allowing `authors` to read from `books`

```
---
apiVersion: policy.linkerd.io/v1beta1
kind: Server
metadata:
  namespace: booksapp
  name: books
  labels:
    app: books
    app.kubernetes.io/part-of: booksapp
    project: booksapp
spec:
  podSelector:
    matchLabels:
      app: books
      project: booksapp
  port: service
  proxyProtocol: HTTP/1
---
apiVersion: policy.linkerd.io/v1beta1
kind: HTTPRoute
metadata:
  name: books-get-route
  namespace: booksapp
  labels:
    app.kubernetes.io/part-of: booksapp
    project: booksapp
spec:
  parentRefs:
    - name: books
      kind: Server
      group: policy.linkerd.io
  rules:
    - matches:
      - path:
          value: "/books.json"
        method: GET
```

```
      - path:
          value: "/books/"
          type: "PathPrefix"
        method: GET
---
apiVersion: policy.linkerd.io/v1alpha1
kind: AuthorizationPolicy
metadata:
  name: allow-authors-to-books
  namespace: booksapp
  labels:
    app.kubernetes.io/part-of: booksapp
    project: booksapp
spec:
  targetRef:
    group: policy.linkerd.io
    kind: HTTPRoute
    name: books-get-route
  requiredAuthenticationRefs:
    - name: authors
      kind: MeshTLSAuthentication
      group: policy.linkerd.io
---
apiVersion: policy.linkerd.io/v1alpha1
kind: MeshTLSAuthentication
metadata:
  name: authors
  namespace: booksapp
spec:
  identities:
    - "authors.booksapp.serviceaccount.identity.linkerd.cluster.local"
---
apiVersion: policy.linkerd.io/v1beta1
kind: HTTPRoute
metadata:
  name: authors-probes
  namespace: booksapp
spec:
  parentRefs:
    - name: authors
      kind: Server
      group: policy.linkerd.io
  rules:
    - matches:
      - path:
          value: "/ping"
        method: GET
---
apiVersion: policy.linkerd.io/v1alpha1
kind: AuthorizationPolicy
metadata:
  name: authors-probe
```

```
    namespace: booksapp
spec:
  targetRef:
    group: policy.linkerd.io
    kind: HTTPRoute
    name: authors-probes
  requiredAuthenticationRefs:
    - name: probe-authn
      kind: NetworkAuthentication
      group: policy.linkerd.io
```

Finally, we need to permit `webapp` to talk to both `authors` and `books`. We can use our existing HTTPRoutes here, and we don't need another Server. All we need to do is add new AuthorizationPolicy and MeshTLSAuthentication resources, as shown in Example 9-9.

What's in an Identity?

We could also do this by adding another identity to our existing `authors` and `books` MeshTLSAuthentications. However, the fine granularity available with route-based policy is a major point in its favor, and using a separate AuthorizationPolicy and MeshTLS-Authentication helps preserve that.

Example 9-9. Permitting web access

```
---
apiVersion: policy.linkerd.io/v1alpha1
kind: AuthorizationPolicy
metadata:
  name: allow-webapp-to-books
  namespace: booksapp
  labels:
    app.kubernetes.io/part-of: booksapp
    project: booksapp
spec:
  targetRef:
    group: policy.linkerd.io
    kind: HTTPRoute
    name: authors-get-route
  requiredAuthenticationRefs:
    - name: webapp
      kind: MeshTLSAuthentication
      group: policy.linkerd.io
---
apiVersion: policy.linkerd.io/v1alpha1
kind: AuthorizationPolicy
metadata:
  name: allow-webapp-to-authors
  namespace: booksapp
```

```
      labels:
        app.kubernetes.io/part-of: booksapp
        project: booksapp
spec:
  targetRef:
    group: policy.linkerd.io
    kind: HTTPRoute
    name: authors-get-route
  requiredAuthenticationRefs:
    - name: webapp
      kind: MeshTLSAuthentication
      group: policy.linkerd.io
---
apiVersion: policy.linkerd.io/v1alpha1
kind: MeshTLSAuthentication
metadata:
  name: webapp
  namespace: booksapp
spec:
  identities:
    - "webapp.booksapp.serviceaccount.identity.linkerd.cluster.local"
```

At this point, we should be able to use a web browser to view the booksapp GUI, and
we should be able to read everything, but modify nothing.

Advanced Techniques

In some situations, you might want to combine multiple workloads in a single Server
definition. As long as the workloads all share the same `port` and `proxyProtocol`, you
can do this using the `In` operator of the Kubernetes `podSelector`:

```
---
apiVersion: policy.linkerd.io/v1beta1
kind: Server
metadata:
  namespace: emojivoto
  name: authors-and-books
  labels:
    app.kubernetes.io/part-of: emojivoto
    project: emojivoto
spec:
  podSelector:
    matchExpressions:
    - key: app
      operator: In
      values:
        - authors
        - books
  port: http
  proxyProtocol: HTTP/1
```

Likewise, MeshTLSAuthentications can list multiple identities:

```
---
apiVersion: policy.linkerd.io/v1alpha1
kind: MeshTLSAuthentication
metadata:
  name: webapp-and-traffic
  namespace: booksapp
spec:
  identities:
    - "webapp.booksapp.serviceaccount.identity.linkerd.cluster.local"
    - "traffic.booksapp.serviceaccount.identity.linkerd.cluster.local"
```

And, of course, HTTPRoutes can list multiple matches, as we've seen throughout this chapter.

These advanced techniques sacrifice a certain amount of granularity, but they can make it considerably easier to set up practical Linkerd policies.

Enabling Write Access

The booksapp application is supposed to allow updating both books and authors, so our next task will be to allow writes to the `authors` workload. Once this is done, we'll be able to make changes to our authors (including updates, additions, and deletions), but we still won't be able to change any books.

The way booksapp is built, both `webapp` and `books` need to be able to write to `authors`. We'll start by creating an HTTPRoute, shown in Example 9-10, that describes the kinds of modification requests we want to allow.

Example 9-10. Modification requests to `authors`

```
---
apiVersion: policy.linkerd.io/v1beta1
kind: HTTPRoute
metadata:
  name: authors-modify-route
  namespace: booksapp
spec:
  parentRefs:
    - name: authors
      kind: Server
      group: policy.linkerd.io
  rules:
    - matches:
      - path:
          value: "/authors/"
          type: "PathPrefix"
        method: DELETE
```

```
    - path:
        value: "/authors/"
        type: "PathPrefix"
      method: PUT
    - path:
        value: "/authors.json"
      method: POST
    - path:
        value: "/"
---
```

This HTTPRoute is attached to our existing `authors` Server, because it describes requests being made to the `authors` workload. Given that HTTPRoute, we want to allow both `books` and `webapp` to make those requests, as shown in Example 9-11.

Example 9-11. Permitting modifications

```
---
apiVersion: policy.linkerd.io/v1alpha1
kind: AuthorizationPolicy
metadata:
  name: authors-modify-policy
  namespace: booksapp
spec:
  targetRef:
    group: policy.linkerd.io
    kind: HTTPRoute
    name: authors-modify-route
  requiredAuthenticationRefs:
    - name: webapp-books
      kind: MeshTLSAuthentication
      group: policy.linkerd.io
---
apiVersion: policy.linkerd.io/v1alpha1
kind: MeshTLSAuthentication
metadata:
  name: webapp-books
  namespace: booksapp
spec:
  identities:
    - "webapp.booksapp.serviceaccount.identity.linkerd.cluster.local"
    - "books.booksapp.serviceaccount.identity.linkerd.cluster.local"
```

Here we're using the technique of listing multiple identities in the same MeshTLS-Authentication, since `webapp` and `books` need *exactly* the same permissions in this example.

After all of this is done, we have the policy setup shown in Figure 9-3.

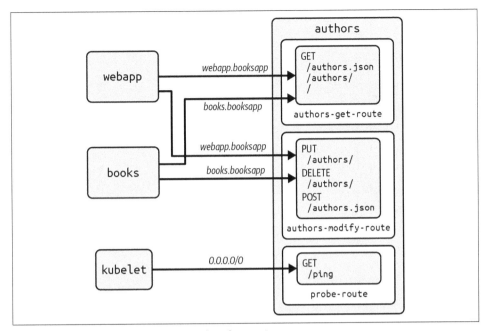

Figure 9-3. books after setting up policy for authors

Allowing Writes to books

We'll finish up our booksapp functionality by allowing writes to the books workload, as shown in Example 9-12. This is exactly parallel to allowing writes to authors and will finally permit booksapp to fully function.

Example 9-12. Modification requests to books

```
---
apiVersion: policy.linkerd.io/v1beta1
kind: HTTPRoute
metadata:
  name: books-modify-route
  namespace: booksapp
spec:
  parentRefs:
    - name: books
      kind: Server
      group: policy.linkerd.io
  rules:
    - matches:
      - path:
          value: "/books/"
          type: "PathPrefix"
        method: DELETE
```

```
      - path:
          value: "/books/"
          type: "PathPrefix"
        method: PUT
      - path:
          value: "/books.json"
        method: POST
      - path:
          value: "/"
---
apiVersion: policy.linkerd.io/v1alpha1
kind: AuthorizationPolicy
metadata:
  name: books-modify-policy
  namespace: booksapp
spec:
  targetRef:
    group: policy.linkerd.io
    kind: HTTPRoute
    name: books-modify-route
  requiredAuthenticationRefs:
    - name: webapp-authors
      kind: MeshTLSAuthentication
      group: policy.linkerd.io
---
apiVersion: policy.linkerd.io/v1alpha1
kind: MeshTLSAuthentication
metadata:
  name: webapp-authors
  namespace: booksapp
spec:
  identities:
    - "webapp.booksapp.serviceaccount.identity.linkerd.cluster.local"
    - "authors.booksapp.serviceaccount.identity.linkerd.cluster.local"
```

Reenabling the Traffic Generator

Finally, we'll add permission for the `traffic` workload, which generates some load at all times, to access the `webapp` workload. The booksapp application doesn't actually need the traffic generator, but it's very useful for debugging and demos! So let's get it running again.

We'll start with a Server for `webapp` (which we haven't needed before), so that we can write policies allowing requests to it. This is shown in Example 9-13.

Example 9-13. A Server for webapp

```
---
apiVersion: policy.linkerd.io/v1beta1
kind: Server
```

```
metadata:
  namespace: booksapp
  name: webapp-server
  labels:
    app: webapp
    app.kubernetes.io/part-of: booksapp
    project: booksapp
spec:
  podSelector:
    matchLabels:
      app: webapp
      project: booksapp
  port: service
  proxyProtocol: HTTP/1
```

Given this Server, it's straightforward to permit `traffic` to access it. We'll take the lazy way out and write a Server-based policy here, as shown in Example 9-14, since we really do want `traffic` to be able to do basically everything.

Example 9-14. Permitting the traffic generator

```
---
apiVersion: policy.linkerd.io/v1alpha1
kind: AuthorizationPolicy
metadata:
  name: allow-traffic
  namespace: booksapp
  labels:
    app.kubernetes.io/part-of: booksapp
    project: booksapp
spec:
  targetRef:
    group: policy.linkerd.io
    kind: Server
    name: webapp
  requiredAuthenticationRefs:
    - name: traffic
      kind: MeshTLSAuthentication
      group: policy.linkerd.io
---
apiVersion: policy.linkerd.io/v1alpha1
kind: MeshTLSAuthentication
metadata:
  name: traffic
  namespace: booksapp
spec:
  identities:
    - "traffic.booksapp.serviceaccount.identity.linkerd.cluster.local"
```

Summary

Linkerd's route-based policy mechanism is the most complex part of Linkerd, enough so that there are actually a number of powerful tools, both open source and commercial, for creating and debugging policies in Linkerd. The Tap component of Linkerd Viz is the simplest, most readily available tool here; likewise, the `linkerd diagnostics` command that we discussed in Chapter 6 has a lot to offer. On the commercial side, we would be remiss if we didn't mention the policy tools available in Buoyant Enterprise for Linkerd.

Overall, policy in Linkerd is a powerful and extensible tool for managing traffic in your cluster, and route-based policy in particular is at once a very powerful mechanism and a very focused tool. It's a great way to further refine policy that you've already established with the Server-based mechanism.

# CHAPTER 10

Observing Your Platform with Linkerd

One of the challenges of working with microservices applications is monitoring them. When dealing with multiple development teams, even in a single language, understanding which workloads are communicating and surfacing useful metrics from those communications can be a huge challenge. Every developer, language, and framework will prioritize different details, and organizations need a single way to view all those different services.

Observability refers to this ability to understand a system by looking at it from the outside. An application can be more or less observable, so when we talk about observability in Linkerd we're referring to how it impacts the observability of your applications. In this chapter, we'll look at how Linkerd increases observability by providing all your apps with standard metrics, allowing you to see the relationships between your microservices, and allowing you to intercept and analyze interapp communications.

Why Do We Need This?

As with application security, microservices present new challenges for platform engineers. The ability to dynamically scale components, create and update services on demand, and dynamically provision infrastructure increases the difficulty of understanding the health of our applications. As your organization builds out your platform for application developers, it's important that you make it easy for teams to do the right thing.

How Does Linkerd Help?

Linkerd helps make observability part of your platform. When you add a workload to the mesh, it begins to automatically surface important information about that workload's behavior. That means that when we add Linkerd to our platform, we make it easy for all our application teams to do the right thing in terms of observability. If you allow your application to join the mesh, you can automatically surface performance, health, and relationship data about your app in a standard way. If you go deeper and build service profiles, you can save and share critical information about the individual routes within your apps.

As we go through this chapter, we'll explore how to observe your applications with Linkerd using the `linkerd` CLI. Everything we cover via the CLI can also be surfaced via the Linkerd Viz dashboard. We'll cover the dashboard near the end of this chapter.

As we mentioned in Chapter 1, there are three golden metrics that have repeatedly proven critical for understanding what's going on in a microservices application: traffic, success rate, and latency (see Figure 1-8).

In a microservices application, having these metrics available for every workload is critical: with just these golden metrics, you should be able to understand how well a given workload is performing as well as what areas of your system need special attention or optimization.

The Linkerd proxy automatically collects detailed metrics from every workload and request and makes them available via Prometheus, so that you can surface this information within your organization using a variety of widely available tools.

Observability in Linkerd

We'll use the booksapp and emojivoto applications to demonstrate observability in Linkerd. Both of these applications deliberately include various failures: we'll use Linkerd observability tools to find where, exactly, the failures are. (Fixing them is left as an exercise for the reader!)

Setting Up Your Cluster

You'll need a cluster with Linkerd and Linkerd Viz already installed (please refer to Chapter 3 if you want a refresher on setting up such a cluster). We'll start by cloning the booksapp sample application (*https://oreil.ly/LJou0*) and emojivoto sample application (*https://oreil.ly/0n5Gd*) repositories, as shown in Example 10-1, since we'll need the repositories to appropriately profile these sample applications.

Example 10-1. Cloning the repos

```
# Clone the booksapp repo
$ git clone https://github.com/BuoyantIO/booksapp.git

# Clone the emojivoto repo
$ git clone https://github.com/BuoyantIO/emojivoto.git
```

Next, we can get the applications up and running in our cluster, as shown in Example 10-2.

Example 10-2. Setting up our apps

```
# Install booksapp
$ kubectl create ns booksapp && \
  curl --proto '=https' --tlsv1.2 -sSfL https://run.linkerd.io/booksapp.yml \
  | linkerd inject - | kubectl -n booksapp apply -f -

# Install emojivoto
$ curl --proto '=https' --tlsv1.2 -sSfL https://run.linkerd.io/emojivoto.yml \
  | linkerd inject - | kubectl apply -f -

# Check that booksapp is ready
$ linkerd check --proxy --namespace booksapp

# Check that emojivoto is ready
$ linkerd check --proxy --namespace emojivoto
```

Once our check returns healthy, we can start looking at our applications using the linkerd viz command, as shown in Example 10-3. Note that it may take a minute or so for Linkerd Viz to start showing any data, since it has to start by collecting enough data to generate statistics.

Example 10-3. Gathering application metrics

```
# View namespace metrics
$ linkerd viz stat ns

# View deployment metrics
$ linkerd viz stat deploy -n emojivoto
$ linkerd viz stat deploy -n booksapp

# View Pod metrics
$ linkerd viz stat pod -n emojivoto
$ linkerd viz stat pod -n booksapp
```

You can immediately see just from these basic queries that the emojivoto and booksapp applications are both having reliability issues. In the following sections, we'll dive deeper into our applications to isolate the source of the problem.

Tap

Linkerd Viz Tap allows authorized users to collect metadata about the requests flowing between your applications. It will surface details about request headers, URIs, response codes, and more, permitting you to access this data on demand for debugging, as shown in Example 10-4. Tap also provides convenient tooling for validating the TLS status of your interapp connections.

Example 10-4. Viewing Tap data

```
# Tap the emojivoto web frontend
$ linkerd viz tap deploy/web -n emojivoto
```

The `linkerd viz tap` command will run until you send it the break signal. It displays live data from the proxy, which will give details about the individual requests that go to and from the web deployment. Each line will show the source and destination details, TLS status, any status information, and other metadata as available.

Installing Tap

Tap is built into the Linkerd Viz extension, so it will be automatically installed by the `linkerd viz install` command. However, if any of your workloads were running before you installed Viz, you'll need to restart those workloads before Tap will be available.

Tap data is a powerful diagnostic tool that can provide insights into how exactly your apps are communicating with one another. If Tap is enabled when you view a workload in the Linkerd Viz dashboard, it will automatically display a summary of requests. Be sure to try to view the Tap data for emojivoto's workloads when you look at the Viz dashboard later in this chapter.

Service Profiles

Linkerd *service profiles*, embodied by the ServiceProfile resource, allow you to give the mesh detailed information about how a given workload is used. At its most basic level, a ServiceProfile defines what routes are allowed for a workload. Once routes are defined, you can configure per-route metrics, timeouts, and retries, as well as which HTTP statuses will be considered failures.

ServiceProfile and HTTPRoute

The Linkerd project is in the midst of a transition to fully adopting Gateway API (*https://oreil.ly/Onjs9*). As the project works toward that objective, you'll see a few Linkerd custom resources, including ServiceProfile, begin to be deprecated.

In Linkerd 2.13 and 2.14, ServiceProfile and HTTPRoute often have mutually exclusive functionality, which makes it particularly important to review the ServiceProfile documentation (*https://oreil.ly/zJk_j*) to verify the current state of ServiceProfile as you begin using these resources in your cluster.

You can build out ServiceProfiles in a number of ways. The most flexible way is to write them by hand, but the Linkerd CLI provides a few different ways to generate them automatically, as you'll see in the following sections.

Configuring routes for emojivoto

The emojivoto application has three workloads:

- The emoji and voting workloads use gRPC for communication, with their gRPC messages defined in protobuf files.

- The web workload uses HTTP to interact with a web browser.

We'll start with emoji and voting, since they have *protobuf* files. Protobuf files work as a guide to our APIs, and they can be consumed by the Linkerd CLI to automatically create ServiceProfiles, as shown in Example 10-5.

Example 10-5. Creating ServiceProfiles from protobuf files

```
# Begin by checking for any existing routes.
$ linkerd viz routes -n emojivoto deploy

# The output will show every workload in the emojivoto
# namespace with a default route. We will now work to
# create application-specific routes for emoji and
# voting.

# Create a ServiceProfile object.
$ linkerd profile --proto emojivoto/proto/Emoji.proto emoji-svc -n emojivoto

# This creates, but doesn't apply, the ServiceProfile
# for the emoji service. Take a minute to review the
# profile object so you understand the basic structure.
# We'll be using these ServiceProfiles again in the
# next chapter.

# Create and apply ServiceProfiles for emoji and voting.
$ linkerd profile --proto emojivoto/proto/Emoji.proto emoji-svc -n emojivoto |
  kubectl apply -f -

$ linkerd profile --proto emojivoto/proto/Voting.proto voting-svc -n emojivoto |
  kubectl apply -f -

# Now you can view the updated route data in your environment to see
# your deployed applications. You may need to wait a minute
# for data to populate.
$ linkerd viz routes deploy/emoji -n emojivoto
$ linkerd viz routes deploy/voting -n emojivoto
```

```
# Each app will show and store details about which routes have
# been accessed.
```

 Storing Linkerd Viz Metrics

Once you've created ServiceProfiles for your applications, Linkerd's Viz extension will store that data in Prometheus. A very important part of taking Linkerd to production is planning how you'll manage this Prometheus data in the long term. The Prometheus component that ships with Linkerd Viz is *not* sufficient for long-term data collection: it stores data in memory, and it *will* lose data every time it restarts.

With our routes created for `emoji` and `voting`, we have two-thirds of our application covered with ServiceProfiles. That leaves the `web` component. Although we know this must speak HTTP because we talk to it with a browser, unfortunately the authors of this component didn't actually write any API documentation for it at all. This leaves us to figure out how to build a ServiceProfile with no information about how the API is structured.

Thankfully, we can use Linkerd's Tap functionality to do just that, as shown in Example 10-6.

Example 10-6. Creating ServiceProfiles with Tap

```
# Create a new ServiceProfile with Tap.
$ linkerd viz profile -n emojivoto web-svc --tap deploy/web --tap-duration 10s |
  kubectl apply -f -

# After you run that command, you should expect to see a
# 10-second pause as Linkerd watches live traffic to the
# service in question and builds a profile.

# View the new profile.
$ kubectl get serviceprofile -n emojivoto web-svc.emojivoto.svc.cluster.local -o yaml

# You will see the object created with two routes, list and vote.

# View the updated route data for web. You may need to allow a minute
# for data to populate.
$ linkerd viz routes deploy/web -n emojivoto
```

Linkerd Default Routes

Linkerd's ServiceProfile objects are intended to define an entire API, but what happens when we make a mistake, or when an API changes without the profiles being updated? That's where the default route comes in: any route that isn't explicitly defined in a ServiceProfile is treated as a default route.

Default routes are subject to default policies regarding retries and timeouts. Data about traffic on default routes is aggregated into the catchall [DEFAULT] route entry.

Building routes for booksapp

Now that we're finished with the emojivoto application, we need to set things up for the booksapp application.

Whereas emojivoto included protobuf files for some of its APIs, booksapp ships with OpenAPI definitions instead. Like protobuf files, OpenAPI definitions (often called "Swagger definitions," after an earlier version of the standard) serve as definitions of how to use the API, and Linkerd knows how to read them to create ServiceProfiles.

Creating a ServiceProfile with an OpenAPI or Swagger definition is almost exactly like creating a ServiceProfile from a protobuf file, as shown in Example 10-7. Please be sure to follow along, as we'll be using these ServiceProfiles again in Chapter 11!

Example 10-7. Creating ServiceProfiles with OpenAPI definitions

```
# Create routes for booksapp.
$ linkerd profile --open-api booksapp/swagger/authors.swagger authors -n booksapp |
  kubectl apply -f -

$ linkerd profile --open-api booksapp/swagger/webapp.swagger webapp -n booksapp |
  kubectl apply -f -

$ linkerd profile --open-api booksapp/swagger/books.swagger books -n booksapp |
  kubectl apply -f -

# With that, we've profiled our applications. We can now wait a minute
# and view the relevant route information.

# View route data for booksapp.
$ linkerd viz routes deploy -n booksapp

# You should see a number of routes with varying success rates.
# In Chapter 11 we'll use some of Linkerd's reliability
# features to help address the issues booksapp is having.
```

Topology

With routes, metrics, and Tap data, we have a lot of useful ways to understand what our apps are doing without requiring developers to include instrumentation in their applications. Another common challenge is figuring out which of all these possible calls are actually happening in the application, and from which workload to which workload. Linkerd can also surface that information for you.

In Example 10-8, we'll examine the relationships between the components of the booksapp application. You can, and should, try to explore emojivoto on your own.

Example 10-8. Viewing edges in Linkerd

```
# Start by getting the deployments in the booksapp namespace.
$ kubectl get deploy -n booksapp

# You'll see four deployments: traffic, webapp, authors, and books.

# Now, dig into the relationship between these components with
# the linkerd viz edges command.
$ linkerd viz edges deploy -n booksapp
```

The output is broken up into five columns:

SRC
> The source of the traffic

DST
> The destination of the traffic

SRC_NS
> The namespace where the traffic originated

DST_NS
> The namespace where the traffic went

SECURED
> Whether or not the traffic is encrypted via Linkerd's mTLS

The resulting output gives you an overview of the relationships between the booksapp components. It shows that the Prometheus instance in the `linkerd-viz` namespace is talking to each deployment in the `booksapp` namespace. Beyond that, we can see that `traffic` talks to `webapp`, `webapp` talks to `books` and `authors`, and `books` and `authors` talk to each other.

The `linkerd viz edges` command will work for Pods or any other workload type within Kubernetes.

Linkerd Viz

You've likely noticed that a number of the commands we used in this chapter were linkerd viz commands. This is the Linkerd Viz extension that we introduced back in Chapter 2. It ships with the core Linkerd system because it's often extremely useful, but it was split out from the core into an extension in Linkerd 2.10, so that not everyone is forced to run it.

The Viz extension provides a great many CLI tools for observing your Linkerd installation, along with a web-based dashboard that provides a graphical interface for exploring your Linkerd environment.

Protecting the Viz Dashboard Is Up to You

As described in Chapter 2, there's no user authentication built into the Linkerd Viz dashboard. You'll need to tackle that using an API gateway or the like if you want to expose Linkerd Viz to the network—or, alternatively, leave the dashboard inaccessible from outside the cluster, and simply use the linkerd viz dashboard CLI command to bring up the dashboard in a web browser, via a port forward.

Use the following command to open the Viz dashboard:

```
$ linkerd viz dashboard
```

Now explore it on your own. Try to find the per-namespace and per-workload metrics. Also take a look at an individual namespace, like emojivoto, and explore the topology.

Linkerd's Viz dashboard includes Prometheus and can easily work with Grafana, as shown in Example 10-9. As we've said a few times before, it's *critical* to realize that the default Linkerd Viz install will create an in-memory Prometheus instance that is *only* viable for demo purposes, and *must not* be relied upon for production use. We recommend you use a separate Prometheus instance for collecting your Linkerd metrics.

Linkerd and Grafana

In earlier versions of Linkerd, linkerd viz install automatically installed Grafana. As of Linkerd 2.12, Grafana licensing changes mean that we're no longer allowed to do that. Grafana still works beautifully with Linkerd Viz, but for Linkerd 2.12 and later you need to install it by hand and configure it to talk to the same Prometheus that Linkerd Viz uses.

Example 10-9. Production-ready Linkerd Viz install

```
# The first step of a production-ready Viz dashboard install
# involves installing a standalone Prometheus instance.
# This guide assumes you've done that in the linkerd-viz
# namespace.

# With that done, you can install Grafana.
$ helm repo add grafana https://grafana.github.io/helm-charts
$ helm repo update
$ helm install grafana -n grafana --create-namespace grafana/grafana \
  -f https://raw.githubusercontent.com/linkerd/linkerd2/main/grafana/values.yaml

# The example install uses a values file provided by the
# Linkerd team. It includes important configurations that
# allow the dashboard to properly use Grafana. You can
# read more in the official Linkerd docs:
# https://linkerd.io/2/tasks/grafana/

# After Grafana is installed, install Linkerd Viz and
# tell it to use your Grafana instance.
$ linkerd viz install --set grafana.url=grafana.grafana:3000 \
  | kubectl apply -f -
```

Audit Trails and Access Logs

Hardening our environments against intrusion doesn't end at reducing the risk and impact of an incident. Having a strong security posture also means being able to rapidly detect when something abnormal has occurred and providing data that allows your security team to understand exactly what you have in place. For Linkerd, much of this data is contained in the system logs of the control plane containers, accessible via kubectl log. It's definitely worth ensuring that you have a strategy for collecting and analyzing log messages that is accessible to your security team.

Beyond normal log messages and events, some users need a detailed history of all the HTTP requests that transit the proxy. This requires *access logging*.

Access Logging: The Good, the Bad, and the Ugly

Access logging in Linkerd means the proxy will write a log message for every HTTP request it processes. In an environment where you have a number of services talking to each other, that can very quickly turn into a huge volume of log messages, so it's definitely worth checking the official Linkerd docs (*https://oreil.ly/zEFj_*) before you implement access logging. We will go into the high-level concepts and practical steps, but the logs are an area where things can change between versions of Linkerd, so be sure to test your setup after looking over the docs.

The good

Access logging will give you hugely detailed information about the interactions between your applications. It is configurable; you can emit the messages in either apache or json format so that they're easier to consume programmatically. With access logging enabled, your security teams will have tremendous amounts of data to help them understand the impact and extent of any security incident.

The bad

Storing and processing these logs is expensive, requires significant engineering overhead, and uses up significant resources in your cluster. Your platform or security teams will need to manage log aggregation tooling and log collection agents on your clusters. Access logging will increase the costs of running your platform.

The ugly

HTTP access logging is disabled by default in Linkerd because it has a performance impact on the proxies in terms of both CPU and latency. That means your application response times and compute costs will increase when you enable it. To what extent will depend very much on your level and type of traffic.

Enabling Access Logging

You can set the access logging configuration at the workload, namespace, or Pod level. In any case, you'll need to set the following annotation:

```
config.linkerd.io/access-log: apache
```

Or:

```
config.linkerd.io/access-log: json
```

After it's set, you need to restart the targeted workloads to begin collecting logs.

We recommend that you test the performance impacts of enabling access logging in your application before rolling it out to production. That will give your organization the data it needs to make an informed decision about access logging in Linkerd.

Summary

Observability in Linkerd ranges from simple metrics to access logging. Linkerd allows us to understand the behavior, performance, and characteristics of our apps without requiring application developers to make any modifications. The power of a service mesh lies in allowing the platform team to provide observability to app teams as a feature of the platform. It also ensures that all apps can be understood and compared in a uniform fashion.

CHAPTER 11
Ensuring Reliability with Linkerd

As discussed from the very beginning, back in Chapter 1, microservices applications are utterly reliant on the network for all of their communications. Networks are slower and less reliable than in-process communication, which introduces new failure modes and presents new challenges to our applications.

For service mesh users, where the mesh mediates all your application traffic, the reliability benefit is that the mesh can make intelligent choices about what to do when things go wrong. In this chapter, we'll talk about the mechanisms that Linkerd provides to mitigate the problems of unreliability in the network, helping to address the inherent instability of microservices applications.

Load Balancing

Load balancing might seem like an odd reliability feature to lead with, since many people think that Kubernetes already handles it. As we first discussed in Chapter 5, Kubernetes Services make a distinction between the IP address of the Service and the IP addresses of the Pods associated with the Service. When traffic is sent to the ClusterIP, it ends up being redirected to one of the endpoint IPs.

However, in Kubernetes, the built-in load balancing is limited to entire connections. Linkerd improves on this by using the proxy, which understands more about the protocol involved in the connection, to choose an endpoint for each request, as shown in Figure 11-1.

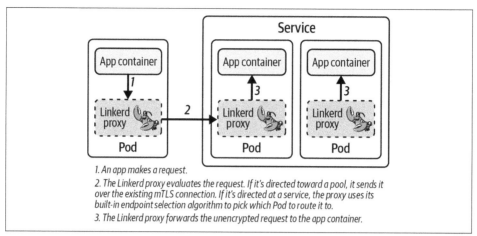

1. An app makes a request.
2. The Linkerd proxy evaluates the request. If it's directed toward a pool, it sends it over the existing mTLS connection. If it's directed at a service, the proxy uses its built-in endpoint selection algorithm to pick which Pod to route it to.
3. The Linkerd proxy forwards the unencrypted request to the app container.

Figure 11-1. Service discovery in Linkerd

As you can see from Figure 11-1, Linkerd will use the destination address from a given request and, depending on the object type it refers to, will adjust its endpoint selection algorithm to select a target.

Request-Level Load Balancing

This distinction between connection-level load balancing and request-level load balancing is more important than it might appear at first glance. Under the hood, Linkerd actually maintains a pool of connections between your workloads, letting it rapidly dispatch requests to whichever workload it thinks appropriate without connection overhead, load balancing the individual requests so that the load is evenly and efficiently distributed.

You can learn more about connection-level load balancing in Kubernetes on the Kubernetes blog (*https://oreil.ly/FMALe*).

The aptly named destination controller in the Linkerd control plane makes this all possible. For each service in the mesh, it maintains a list of the service's current endpoints as well as their health and relative performance. The Linkerd proxy uses that information to make intelligent decisions about where and how to send a given request.

Retries

Sometimes, due to network issues or intermittent application failures, a request might fail. In this situation, the Linkerd proxy can *retry* the request for you, automatically repeating it to give the workload another chance to handle it successfully. Of course, it's not always safe to retry every request, so the Linkerd proxy will only do automatic retries if you've explicitly configured retries for a given route, and you should only configure retries when you know they're safe.

Don't Blindly Retry!

Think before you enable retries for a particular request! Not all requests can be safely retried—consider a request that withdraws money from an account, and imagine retrying it in a scenario where the request succeeds but somehow the response gets lost, or the withdrawal service crashes before it can send a reply but after the money is moved. This is not a request that should be retried.

Retry Budgets

Many service meshes and API gateways use *counted retries*, where you define a maximum number of times a request can be retried before a failure is returned to the caller. Linkerd, by contrast, uses *budgeted retries*, where retrying continues as long as the ratio of retries to original requests doesn't exceed the budget.

By default, the budget is 20%, plus 10 more "free" retries per second, averaged over 10 seconds. For example, if your workload is taking 100 requests per second (RPS), then Linkerd would allow adding 30 more retries per second (20% of 100 is 20, plus an additional 10).

Budgeted Retries Versus Counted Retries

Linkerd uses budgeted retries because they tend to let you more directly control the thing you really care about: how much extra load will retries add to the system? Usually, choosing a specific number of retries doesn't really help control load: if you're taking 10 RPS and allow 3 retries, you're up to 40 RPS, but if you're at 100 RPS and allow 3 retries, you might be up to *400* RPS. Budgeted retries control the added load much more directly, while also tending to avoid the retry storms that can happen under high load (where large amounts of retries can themselves crash a Pod, thus causing more retries…).

Configuring Retries

Take a minute to examine the traffic from books to authors using `linkerd viz`:

```
$ linkerd viz -n booksapp routes deploy/books --to svc/authors
```

You'll see that the books workload is only sending requests to a single route over on the authors service: `HEAD /authors/{id}.json`. Those requests are failing half the time, making them a great candidate for retries—HEAD requests are always idempotent (that is, they can always be repeated without the result changing), so we can always safely enable retries on that route.

In Linkerd, we control retry behavior with ServiceProfile resources. In this case, we'll be using the ServiceProfile for the `authors` service, since we're going to enable retries when talking *to* the `authors` workload.

Retries, ServiceProfiles, HTTPRoutes, and Linkerd

As mentioned earlier, the Linkerd project is in the midst of a transition to fully adopting Gateway API (*https://oreil.ly/a-Xug*), which means you'll soon see a few Linkerd custom resources, including ServiceProfile, begin to be deprecated.

In Linkerd 2.13 and 2.14, ServiceProfile and HTTPRoute often have mutually exclusive functionality, which makes it particularly important to review the retry and timeout documentation (*https://oreil.ly/1EPEX*) to verify the current state of ServiceProfile as you begin building retries into your applications.

Start by looking at the existing ServiceProfile using `kubectl get`:

```
$ kubectl get serviceprofile -n booksapp \
    authors.booksapp.svc.cluster.local
```

This ServiceProfile should look a lot like the one in Example 11-1.

Example 11-1. The `authors` ServiceProfile

```
apiVersion: linkerd.io/v1alpha2
kind: ServiceProfile
metadata:
  name: authors.booksapp.svc.cluster.local
  namespace: booksapp
spec:
  routes:
  - condition:
      method: GET
      pathRegex: /authors\.json
    name: GET /authors.json
  - condition:
      method: POST
      pathRegex: /authors\.json
    name: POST /authors.json
  - condition:
      method: DELETE
      pathRegex: /authors/[^/]*\.json
    name: DELETE /authors/{id}.json
```

```
  - condition:
      method: GET
      pathRegex: /authors/[^/]*\.json
    name: GET /authors/{id}.json
  - condition:
      method: HEAD
      pathRegex: /authors/[^/]*\.json
    name: HEAD /authors/{id}.json
```

You can see five routes listed in the ServiceProfile. We're going to focus on the last route, HEAD /authors/{id}.json.

We can configure retries independently for each route by adding the isRetryable: true property to the ServiceProfile entry for the route. In addition to that, each ServiceProfile object can define the retry budget for the all the routes in the Service-Profile.

The easiest way to add this property is to interactively edit the ServiceProfile:

```
$ kubectl edit serviceprofiles authors.booksapp.svc.cluster.local -n booksapp
```

Use your editor to change the ServiceProfile so that the HEAD /authors/{id}.json route has the isRetryable property set to true, as shown in Example 11-2.

Example 11-2. The authors ServiceProfile with retries

```
apiVersion: linkerd.io/v1alpha2
kind: ServiceProfile
metadata:
  name: authors.booksapp.svc.cluster.local
  namespace: booksapp
spec:
  routes:
  - condition:
      method: GET
      pathRegex: /authors\.json
    name: GET /authors.json
  - condition:
      method: POST
      pathRegex: /authors\.json
    name: POST /authors.json
  - condition:
      method: DELETE
      pathRegex: /authors/[^/]*\.json
    name: DELETE /authors/{id}.json
  - condition:
      method: GET
      pathRegex: /authors/[^/]*\.json
    name: GET /authors/{id}.json
  - condition:
      method: HEAD
```

```
    pathRegex: /authors/[^/]*\.json
    name: HEAD /authors/{id}.json
    isRetryable: true
```

Save your changes to the `authors` ServiceProfile and examine the routes using `linkerd viz routes` once again, as shown here:

```
$ linkerd viz -n booksapp routes deploy/books --to svc/authors -o wide
```

Switching the output format using `-o wide` tells the `linkerd viz routes` command to show the effective success rate (after retries) as well as the actual success rate (before retries are taken into consideration). If you run this command repeatedly after enabling retries, you'll see that the effective success rate will climb as the overall latency goes up. Over time, the effective success rate should climb to 100%, even though the actual success rate stays consistent at about 50%: the `authors` workload is still failing about half the time, even though retries are able to mask that from the caller.

The watch Command

If you have the `watch` command, this is a great time to use it. It will rerun the command every two seconds until interrupted, giving you an easy way to see things changing:

```
$ watch linkerd viz -n booksapp \
    routes deploy/books --to svc/authors -o wide
```

You can also see the difference in the effective and actual RPS. The effective RPS is about 2.2, but the actual RPS will hover near double that—that's because *retries add load to the failing service* by making additional requests to mask the failures.

Why Are We Seeing a Factor of Two?

We often quote the default retry budget as 20%—so how is it possible that we're seeing twice the traffic in this situation? For that matter, how is it possible that we're seeing Linkerd mask all the failures when *50% of requests are failing?*

The answer to both questions lies with the "free" 10 requests per second included in the default budget. Since the actual load is significantly less than 10 RPS, the extra 10 "free" requests per second are plenty to effectively allow retrying 100% of the actual traffic, permitting Linkerd to mask all the failures…at the cost of doubling the traffic.

Those "free" 10 RPS also mean that you don't have to worry about Linkerd's budget letting failures leak through on a lightly used service, even while the budget protects you from retry storms on a heavily used service.

Configuring the Budget

Linkerd's default budget actually works out well for many applications, but if you need to change it, you'll need to edit the `retryBudget` stanza in your ServiceProfile, as shown in Example 11-3.

Example 11-3. An example retry budget

```
...
spec:
  ...
  # This retryBudget stanza is AN EXAMPLE ONLY
  retryBudget:
    retryRatio: 0.3
    minRetriesPerSecond: 50
    ttl: 60s
  ...
```

The `retryBudget` stanza shown in Example 11-3 would allow retrying 30% of original requests, plus *50* "free" requests per second, averaged over a full minute.

Don't Blindly Use This Budget!

The budget shown in Example 11-3 is *just an example*. Please do not assume that it will be helpful for any actual application!

Timeouts

Timeouts are a tool that allows us to force a failure in the event a given request is taking too long. They're particularly effective when used hand-in-hand with retries, so that a request that takes too long will be retried—but you don't have to use them together! There are a lot of situations where a judiciously placed timeout can help return agency to an application, opening the door to providing a better user experience by making intelligent decisions about what to do if things are slow.

When timeouts are configured and a request takes too long, the Linkerd proxy will return an HTTP 504 for the request. The timeout will look like any other request failure as far as Linkerd's observability functionality is concerned (including triggering a retry, if retries are enabled), and it will be counted toward the effective failure rate on a given route.

Configuring Timeouts

Let's start things off by taking a look at requests from webapp to books, to see what the average latency for user requests looks like:

```
$ linkerd viz -n booksapp routes deploy/webapp --to svc/books
```

Let's focus on the PUT /books/{id}.json route. Latency varies from environment to environment, but we'll start with a latency of 25 ms for our example; this will probably result in some timeouts being triggered in most environments. You can use the resulting success rates to tune the timeouts in your cluster.

Just like retries, timeouts are configured via ServiceProfiles in Linkerd. As we did with retries, we'll start by looking at the existing profile. We can get the books ServiceProfile with this command:

```
$ kubectl get sp/books.booksapp.svc.cluster.local -n booksapp -o yaml
```

This ServiceProfile should look very similar to the one in Example 11-4.

Example 11-4. The books ServiceProfile

```yaml
apiVersion: linkerd.io/v1alpha2
kind: ServiceProfile
metadata:
  name: books.booksapp.svc.cluster.local
  namespace: booksapp
spec:
  routes:
  - condition:
      method: GET
      pathRegex: /books\.json
    name: GET /books.json
  - condition:
      method: POST
      pathRegex: /books\.json
    name: POST /books.json
  - condition:
      method: DELETE
      pathRegex: /books/[^/]*\.json
    name: DELETE /books/{id}.json
  - condition:
      method: GET
      pathRegex: /books/[^/]*\.json
    name: GET /books/{id}.json
  - condition:
      method: PUT
      pathRegex: /books/[^/]*\.json
    name: PUT /books/{id}.json
```

We configure timeouts by adding the `timeout` property to a route entry, setting its value to a time specification that can be parsed by Go's `time.ParseDuration`.

Timeouts, ServiceProfiles, HTTPRoutes, and Linkerd

As mentioned earlier, the Linkerd project is in the midst of a transition to fully adopting Gateway API (*https://oreil.ly/6XTtV*), so a few Linkerd custom resources, including ServiceProfile, will soon begin to be deprecated.

ServiceProfile and HTTPRoute have overlapping functionality for timeouts starting with Gateway API 1.0.0, which at the time of writing is not yet supported by a stable Linkerd version. It's particularly important to review the retry and timeout documentation (*https://oreil.ly/41V-2*) to verify the current state of ServiceProfile as you begin building retries into your applications.

One particular note is that the syntax for HTTPRoute timeouts, specified by GEP-2257 (*https://oreil.ly/lxLGa*), is rather more restrictive than Go's `time.ParseDuration`, which is used for ServiceProfile timeouts. For maximum compatibility in the future, you may want to consider updating your ServiceProfile timeouts to conform to GEP-2257.

The simplest way to add a timeout to the `PUT /books/{id}.json` route is to edit the ServiceProfile interactively, which you can do using the following command:

```
$ kubectl edit serviceprofiles.linkerd.io \
    books.booksapp.svc.cluster.local -n booksapp
```

You will need to add the `timeout` element to the `PUT /books/{id}.json` route, with a value of `25ms`. This is shown in Example 11-5.

Example 11-5. The books *ServiceProfile with a timeout*

```
apiVersion: linkerd.io/v1alpha2
kind: ServiceProfile
metadata:
  name: books.booksapp.svc.cluster.local
  namespace: booksapp
spec:
  routes:
  - condition:
      method: GET
      pathRegex: /books\.json
    name: GET /books.json
  - condition:
      method: POST
      pathRegex: /books\.json
```

```
    name: POST /books.json
  - condition:
      method: DELETE
      pathRegex: /books/[^/]*\.json
    name: DELETE /books/{id}.json
  - condition:
      method: GET
      pathRegex: /books/[^/]*\.json
    name: GET /books/{id}.json
  - condition:
      method: PUT
      pathRegex: /books/[^/]*\.json
    name: PUT /books/{id}.json
    timeout: 25ms
```

With the timeout set, you'll want to observe the traffic going from the webapp to the books service to see how the timeout is impacting the overall availability of your service. Once again, linkerd viz routes is one of the simplest ways to do this:

```
$ linkerd viz -n booksapp routes deploy/webapp --to svc/books
```

(You can use -o wide if you want—it won't directly help you when observing latency, but it's certainly not harmful.)

Timeouts provide a valuable tool to ensure the overall availability of your applications. They allow you to control latency and ensure applications don't hang while waiting for responses from downstream services.

Traffic Shifting

Traffic shifting refers to changing the destination of a request based on outside criteria. Typically this is a weighted split between two or more destinations (a *canary*), or a split based on a header match, username, etc. (an *A/B split*), although many other types are possible. Traffic shifting is a major part of progressive delivery, where you roll out new application versions by carefully shifting traffic to the new version and verifying functionality as you go. However, you needn't do progressive delivery to benefit from traffic shifting.

Traffic Shifting, Gateway API, and the Linkerd SMI Extension

As of Linkerd 2.13, Linkerd natively supports traffic shifting using the Gateway API HTTPRoute resource, so traffic shifting is the first area where we'll use Gateway API resources to configure Linkerd.

HTTPRoutes Versus Linkerd SMI

In Linkerd versions prior to 2.13, you can still do traffic shifting, but you need to use the Linkerd SMI extension (which we mentioned in Chapter 2). For information about the SMI extension and its legacy TrafficSplit resources, check out the official Linkerd docs on SMI (*https://oreil.ly/56HlN*). We recommend using Gateway API in 2.13 and later, though.

As we explore traffic shifting in Linkerd, we'll look at the two basic ways of doing it: weight-based and header-based.

Setting Up Your Environment

In this section we'll be demonstrating traffic shifting using an entirely different application called podinfo (*https://oreil.ly/1IL4K*). To follow along with the traffic shifting demos, we recommend you start a new cluster; please refer to the material in Chapter 3 if you need any help with that.

Once you have your new cluster, you can follow along with Example 11-6 to get started shifting traffic with podinfo.

Example 11-6. Launching podinfo

```
# Start in a clean working directory, as we will be cloning the
# linkerd-book/luar Git repository.
$ git clone https://github.com/linkerd-book/luar.git

# First, we'll create our namespace, podinfo, with the
# linkerd.io/inject: enabled annotation set on it. This will
# ensure our Pods get Linkerd proxies attached to them.
$ kubectl apply -f luar/reliability/ns.yaml

# Next, we'll install the podinfo application using Helm.
$ helm repo add podinfo https://stefanprodan.github.io/podinfo
$ helm repo up

# Install 3 versions of podinfo:
# - podinfo is our "version 1" Pod.
# - podinfo-2 is our "version 2" Pod.
# - frontend is a frontend to the whole thing.
$ helm install podinfo \
    --namespace podinfo \
    --set ui.message="hello from v1" \
    podinfo/podinfo
```

```
$ helm install podinfo-2 \
    --namespace podinfo \
    --set ui.message="hello from v2" \
    podinfo/podinfo

$ helm install frontend \
    --namespace podinfo \
    --set backend=http://podinfo:9898/env \
    podinfo/podinfo

# Create a traffic generator for podinfo.
$ kubectl apply -f luar/reliability/generator.yaml

# Check that the applications are ready.
$ linkerd check --proxy -n podinfo

# Verify that both versions of the podinfo workload are running.
$ kubectl get pods -n podinfo

# Verify that each version of podinfo has its own Service.
$ kubectl get svc -n podinfo
```

With that, we have our base demo application ready for traffic splitting. The basic layout of our application is shown in Figure 11-2.

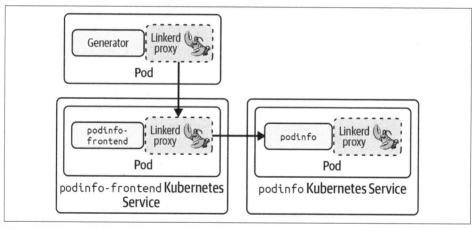

Figure 11-2. podinfo application architecture

Next, you'll want to watch how traffic is moving through your cluster. It's best to start this running in a separate window, as shown in Example 11-7, so you can see what changes as you manipulate resources.

Example 11-7. Watching podinfo traffic

```
# If you have the watch command, it works well for this.
$ watch linkerd viz stat deploy -n podinfo

# If you don't have watch, it's simple enough to emulate.
$ while true; do
  clear
  date
  linkerd viz stat deploy -n podinfo
  sleep 2
done
```

This will show you how traffic is being routed in your cluster. You should see two podinfo deployments, `podinfo` and `podinfo-v2`. `podinfo-v2` should be receiving very little traffic at the moment since we haven't yet shifted any traffic to it.

Weight-Based Routing (Canary)

Weight-based routing is a method of shifting traffic that selects where a given request will go based on simple percentages: a certain percentage of available traffic goes to one destination, and the rest goes to another. Weight-based routing allows us to shift a small percentage of traffic to the new version of a service to see how it behaves.

In progressive delivery this is called *canary routing*, named after the proverbial "canary in a coal mine" that would warn miners when the air was going bad by dying. Here, the idea is that you can shift a small amount of traffic to test if the new version of your workload will die, or work, before you shift more traffic. A successful canary ends when all the traffic has been shifted and the old version can be retired.

To start the canary running, we'll need to create an HTTPRoute, as shown in Example 11-8.

Which HTTPRoute?

We're going to use `policy.linkerd.io` HTTPRoutes to accommodate readers with older versions of Linkerd. It's important to be aware, though, that tools like Flagger and Argo Rollouts *do not* support `policy.linkerd.io`! If you're using one of these tools, you'll need to use the `gateway.networking.k8s.io` HTTPRoutes, which requires Linkerd 2.14 or higher.

Example 11-8. The canary HTTPRoute

```
---
apiVersion: policy.linkerd.io/v1beta2
kind: HTTPRoute
metadata:
  name: podinfo-route
  namespace: podinfo
spec:
  parentRefs:
    - name: podinfo
      namespace: podinfo
      kind: Service
      group: core
      port: 9898
  rules:
  - backendRefs:
    - name: podinfo
      namespace: podinfo
      port: 9898
      weight: 5
    - name: podinfo-v2
      namespace: podinfo
      port: 9898
      weight: 5
```

This HTTPRoute will split traffic between the `podinfo` and `podinfo-v2` services. We set the weight to 5 for both services, which will cause 50% of the traffic to shift over to `podinfo-v2`, while leaving 50% with our original `podinfo`.

The Ratio Is What Matters

The absolute values of the weights don't usually matter—they don't need to add up to any particular number. What does matter is the *ratio* of weights, so using weights of 5 and 5, or 100 and 100, or 1 and 1 would all give 50/50 splits.

On the other hand, a weight of 0 explicitly means *not* to direct any traffic to that backend—so don't try to use 0/0 for a 50/50 split.

Service versus Service: ClusterIPs, endpoints, and HTTPRoutes

The astute reader will notice that we're using `podinfo` twice: once in `parentRefs` and once in `backendRefs`. Won't this cause a routing loop? Aren't we arranging for traffic to come to `podinfo`, then get directed to `podinfo` again, and do this forever until eventually it finally gets shuffled to `podinfo-v2`?

Rest assured that that won't happen. If we go back to the Kubernetes Service architecture shown in Figure 11-3, the critical bits are that:

- When a Service is used in `parentRefs`, it means that the HTTPRoute will control traffic directed to the Service.

- When a Service is used in `backendRefs`, it allows the HTTPRoute to direct traffic to the Pods attached to the Service.

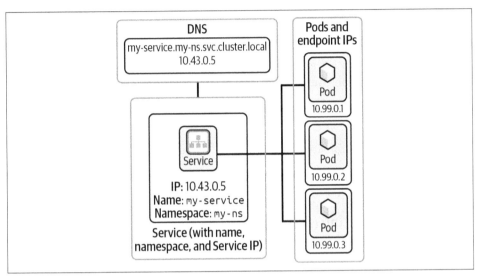

Figure 11-3. The three distinct parts of a Kubernetes Service

So what we're really saying with `podinfo-route` is that 95% of the traffic to the podinfo Service IP will be directed to the `podinfo` *endpoints*, and the other 5% will be directed to the `podinfo-v2` *endpoints*, so there are no loops. This behavior is defined in GEP-1426 (*https://oreil.ly/uYWpL*) from the GAMMA initiative.

You Can't Route to a Route

GEP-1426 also prevents HTTPRoutes from "stacking." Suppose that we apply `podinfo-route` as shown in Example 11-8, then also apply another HTTPRoute (`podinfo-v2-canary`) that tries to split traffic to `podinfo-v2`. In that case:

- Traffic sent directly to `podinfo-v2` *will* be split by `podinfo-v2-canary`.

- Traffic sent to `podinfo` that `podinfo-route` then directs to `podinfo-v2` will *not* be split.

This is because `podinfo-route` will send its traffic directly to the `podinfo-v2` *endpoints*. Since that traffic bypasses the `podinfo-v2` Service IP, `podinfo-v2-canary` never gets a chance to work with it.

Apply `podinfo-route` to your cluster and take a look at how the traffic shifts in your terminal window that's watching traffic. You'll see around 25 requests per second going to the v2 deployment (remember that it will take a little time for the metrics that `linkerd viz` is watching to catch up).

You can modify the weights and see how traffic shifts around in real time: just use `kubectl edit` as shown here:

```
$ kubectl edit httproute -n podinfo podinfo-route
```

As soon as you save an edited version, the new weights should instantly take effect, changing what you see in your window that's watching traffic.

Once you're finished, go ahead and delete the `podinfo-route` route, using the following command:

```
$ kubectl delete httproute -n podinfo podinfo-route
```

You should see all the traffic shifting back to `podinfo`, setting the stage for our header-based routing experiment.

Header-Based Routing (A/B Testing)

Header-based routing allows you to make routing decisions based on the headers included in a request. This is commonly used for A/B testing. For example, if you have two versions of a user interface, you typically don't want to randomly choose between them every time your user loads a page. Instead, you might use some header that identifies the user to pick a version of the UI in a deterministic way, so that a given user will always see a consistent UI, but different users might get different UIs.

We'll use header-based routing to allow selecting a version of `podinfo` using a header. Start by applying a new `podinfo-route` HTTPRoute, as shown in Example 11-9. (Once again, we're going to use `policy.linkerd.io` HTTPRoutes; see "Which HTTPRoute?" on page 165 for a caveat on this choice.)

Example 11-9. Header-based routing

```
apiVersion: policy.linkerd.io/v1beta2
kind: HTTPRoute
metadata:
  name: podinfo-route
  namespace: podinfo
spec:
  parentRefs:
    - name: podinfo
      kind: Service
      group: core
      port: 9898
  rules:
```

```
    - matches:
      - headers:
        - name: "x-request-id"
          value: "alternative"
      backendRefs:
        - name: "podinfo-v2"
          port: 9898
    - backendRefs:
      - name: "podinfo"
        port: 9898
```

(If you were just following the instructions for weight-based routing, that's fine; this `podinfo-route` will overwrite the one from that section if you didn't already delete it.)

This version has a new `matches` section for header matches. We also move the reference to `podinfo-v2` from the main `backendRefs` section to a new `backendRefs` under `matches`. The effect is that traffic will be shifted to `podinfo-v2` only if it has the header `x-request-id` with a value of `alternative`.

Since the traffic generator we installed doesn't send any requests with the correct header, when you apply this HTTPRoute, you should immediately see all the traffic fall away from `podinfo-v2`. We can use `curl` to send traffic with the correct header to be routed to `podinfo-v2`, as shown in Example 11-10.

Example 11-10. Testing header-based routing with `curl`

```
# Start by forwarding traffic to your frontend service.
$ kubectl port-forward svc/frontend-podinfo 9898:9898 &

# Now send a request to the service and see what message you get back.
# You should see "hello from v1" since this request didn't include the
# header.
$ curl -sX POST localhost:9898/echo \
  | jq -r ".[]" | grep MESSAGE

# Now try again, setting the x-request-id header.
# You should see "hello from v2" since this request does include the
# header.
$ curl -H 'x-request-id: alternative' -sX POST localhost:9898/echo \
  | jq -r ".[]" | grep MESSAGE
```

Traffic Shifting Summary

You now have a sense of how to use HTTPRoute objects to manipulate traffic in your cluster. While it's still possible, for the moment, to use the Linkerd SMI extension, we strongly recommend using Gateway API instead—and if you're using Linkerd with a progressive delivery tool like Flagger or Argo Rollouts, using Gateway API can dramatically simplify the interface with that tool (although, as noted earlier, you'll likely need to use Linkerd 2.14 for its support for the official Gateway API types).

Circuit Breaking

When you run applications at scale, it can be helpful to automatically isolate and direct traffic away from any Pod that is experiencing issues. Linkerd tends to route away from underperforming Pods automatically, by virtue of using an exponentially weighted moving average of latency to select the Pod to receive a given request. With circuit breaking, you can make Linkerd explicitly avoid routing to any Pods that are experiencing issues.

Enabling Circuit Breaking

When you enable circuit breaking on a Service, Linkerd will selectively quarantine endpoints that experience multiple consecutive failures. As always with advanced features, make sure you read the latest Linkerd circuit breaking documentation (*https://oreil.ly/33gHv*) before implementing this in your environment.

We'll demonstrate using Linkerd circuit breaking by installing a deliberately bad Pod:

```
$ kubectl apply -f luar/reliability/podinfo-v3.yaml
```

In your terminal that's watching traffic, you should now see three `podinfo` deployments running. Traffic should be roughly evenly split between `podinfo` and `podinfo-v3`, because `podinfo-v3` is carefully set up to be part of the same Service as `podinfo`.

> **Seeing podinfo-v2?**
>
> If you're seeing any traffic to `podinfo-v2`, check to make sure you don't have any HTTPRoutes still splitting traffic by running `kubectl get httproute -n podinfo`.

You should also note that `podinfo-v3` has a less than 100% success rate. Adding a circuit breaker to the `podinfo` Service, as shown here, should improve things:

```
$ kubectl annotate -n podinfo svc/podinfo \
    balancer.linkerd.io/failure-accrual=consecutive
```

This tells Linkerd to apply the circuit breaking policy to the `podinfo` Service. It will look for consecutive failures and stop routing to any Pods that are having issues. If you look back at your window that's watching traffic, you'll soon see that `podinfo-v3` is no longer receiving much traffic.

Why Annotations?

Circuit breakers are still rather new in Linkerd, so they're currently configurable only using annotations. Keep an eye on the latest Linkerd circuit breaking documentation (*https://oreil.ly/bdiFR*) to stay up-to-date as development proceeds!

Tuning Circuit Breaking

We can further tune circuit breaking with additional annotations on the Service:

`balancer.linkerd.io/failure-accrual-consecutive-max-failures`
> Sets the number of failures that you'll need to see before an endpoint is quarantined. Defaults to 7.

`balancer.linkerd.io/failure-accrual-consecutive-min-penalty`
> Sets the minimum time an endpoint should be put in quarantine. GEP-2257 Duration, defaults to one second (`1s`).

`balancer.linkerd.io/failure-accrual-consecutive-max-penalty`
> Sets the upper bound for the quarantine period (the maximum time that an endpoint will be quarantined before the mesh tests it again). GEP-2257 Duration, defaults to one minute (`1m`).

`balancer.linkerd.io/failure-accrual-consecutive-jitter-ratio`
> Adds some randomness to the quarantine and test timeframes. Defaults to `0.5`; tuning is only rarely appropriate.

Looking at the traffic, you'll probably still see `podinfo-v3` showing too many failures. Making it a bit more sensitive to failure, as shown in Example 11-11, will allow the circuit breaker to more aggressively take `podinfo-v3` out of circulation, which should help the situation.

Example 11-11. Tuning circuit breaking

```
# First, we'll set the number of failures we need to see to quarantine
# the endpoints. In this case, we'll change it from the default of 7 to 3.
$ kubectl annotate -n podinfo svc/podinfo \
  balancer.linkerd.io/failure-accrual-consecutive-max-failures=3

# Next, we'll change the minimum quarantine time to 30 seconds from 1 second.
$ kubectl annotate -n podinfo svc/podinfo \
  balancer.linkerd.io/failure-accrual-consecutive-min-penalty=30s

# Finally, we change the max penalty time to 2 minutes.
$ kubectl annotate -n podinfo svc/podinfo \
  balancer.linkerd.io/failure-accrual-consecutive-max-penalty=2m
```

With that, we should see far fewer errors making it through to podinfo-v3.

Circuit Breaking Won't Hide All Failures

When Linkerd checks to see if a given endpoint has recovered, it does so by allowing an actual user request through. If this request fails, the failure will get all the way back to the caller (unless retries are also enabled).

In our example, this would mean that a potentially failing request will make it to podinfo-v3 every 30 seconds, in order for Linkerd to check to see if the circuit breaker can be reset.

Summary

With that, we've covered how Linkerd can help reliability in your applications. You can retry in the event of transient failures in the network and in your APIs, add timeouts to requests to preserve overall availability, split traffic between versions of a service to perform safer rollouts, and set up circuit breakers to protect services from failing Pods. With all this, you're well on your way to being able to run a reliable and resilient platform with Linkerd.

# CHAPTER 12

Multicluster Communication with Linkerd

Every Kubernetes cluster represents a single security and operational failure domain. As you look at scaling out your platform to accommodate more teams, more customers, and more use cases, you will inevitably run into the question of how you want to distribute your apps. Do you want to use large regional clusters with all your production apps in one place? Do you want to use purpose-built clusters for each app or each team? Most teams end up somewhere in the middle, with some shared clusters and some purpose-built for certain apps or categories of apps.

Linkerd aims to make the technical implementation problems around running multiple clusters easier to solve.

Types of Multicluster Setups

Linkerd supports two styles of multicluster configurations: *gateway-based multicluster* and *Pod-to-Pod multicluster*. Gateway-based multicluster setups are easier to deploy; Pod-to-Pod setups offer more advanced functionality. You can choose which is best for a given situation, and you can even use both in the same cluster at the same time, if desired.

Gateway-Based Multicluster

Linkerd's gateway-based multicluster setup routes communications between clusters through a special workload that Linkerd calls a gateway, which is reachable via a LoadBalancer Service. This means that gateway-based multicluster connections don't require any particularly demanding network configuration: all that's required for gateway-based multicluster communications is that Pods in a given cluster can connect to the LoadBalancer of the other cluster's gateway, no matter how that happens.

The network also doesn't need to be secure: Linkerd will take care of that with its usual mTLS.

The gateway-based multicluster architecture is shown in Figure 12-1.

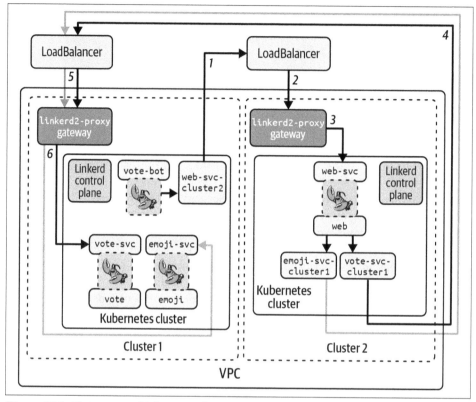

Figure 12-1. Gateway multicluster architecture

The numbers in the diagram show the number of network hops made when the vote-bot in cluster 1 talks to web in cluster 2, which then talks to vote back in cluster 1. (This actually happens in emojivoto.) Following the path, you'll see a total of six hops. This can complicate things sometimes, which led to the development of Pod-to-Pod multicluster.

Pod-to-Pod Multicluster

A Pod-to-Pod multicluster configuration, by contrast, relies on your Pods being able to talk *directly* to each other, even across cluster boundaries. This can be quite a bit more challenging to set up, because your cluster provider needs to be able to support it. If you're creating your own bare-metal clusters, this is probably quite possible. If you're using a cloud provider, it will depend on the provider.

The Pod-to-Pod multicluster architecture is shown in Figure 12-2.

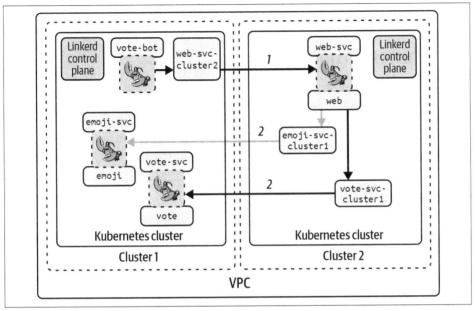

Figure 12-2. Pod-to-Pod multicluster architecture

Following the path from `vote-bot` to `web` and back to `vote` here, we see only two hops, the same as we would see in a single cluster.

Gateways Versus Pod-to-Pod

As with many things in computing, the mode to choose depends on your situation:

- The gateway-based multicluster mode is unquestionably simpler to set up; Pod-to-Pod requires more advanced networking support.
- Pod-to-Pod is marginally faster than gateway-based, since there's no hop through a gateway. With Linkerd this tends to be negligible, though.
- A potentially more important concern is that in a gateway-based multicluster setup, any call from another cluster will appear as having the identity *of the gateway*, not the actual originating workload.
- Another important concern is that in Pod-to-Pod mode, the Linkerd `destination` service also needs to be able to connect to the remote Kubernetes API server.

Remember that the two modes can coexist in the same cluster as long as you have the correct IP connectivity. You have an enormous amount of flexibility in how you work with multicluster communications.

Multicluster Certificates

Whichever kind of multicluster setup you decide to use, your clusters' trust hierarchies need a common root for Linkerd to establish a multicluster connection between clusters. By far the easiest way to do this is to have them share a common trust anchor, as shown in Figure 12-3. This also implies that if you want clusters to be isolated from each other, they *must not* share the same trust anchor!

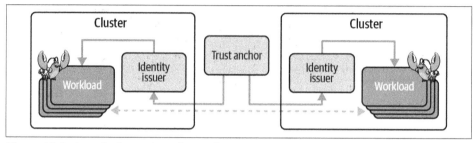

Figure 12-3. A multicluster trust hierarchy

The simplest way to manage this is usually to have a single trust anchor for each environment level (Dev, UAT, Production, Test, etc.), so that, for example, development clusters can peer with each other but not with production clusters. Likewise, it's often simplest to set up a CA for each of these levels, too, so that each CA needs to worry about only one kind of certificate.

Don't Share Identity Issuers

Even in multicluster setups, your clusters should not share identity issuer certificates. Keeping the identity issuers separate is important both for being certain of where a given workload identity originated and for simplifying the operational aspects of rotating the identity issuers.

Ultimately, the needs of your environment will dictate how you set up certificates and CAs.

Cross-Cluster Service Discovery

The last piece of the multicluster puzzle is service discovery: how do workloads in one cluster know where to find workloads in other clusters? Linkerd tackles this problem with the *service mirror*, which is a part of the control plane supplied by the Multicluster extension.

As its name implies, the service mirror arranges for Services in one cluster to appear in other clusters. Exactly how it sets up the mirrored Services depends on the type of multicluster configuration you're using:

Gateway-based multicluster
> Connections to a mirrored Service will be redirected to the gateway in front of the original Service. The gateway then knows how to carry the requests on to a real Pod, including endpoint selection, policy enforcement, etc.

Pod-to-Pod multicluster
> Connections to a mirrored Service will simply transit the network directly to the other Pod. The Linkerd proxy next to the workload making the connection knows which endpoints are available directly, so it handles load balancing, policy enforcement, etc.

The service mirror doesn't blindly mirror every Service; it only mirrors those with a `mirror.linkerd.io/exported` label. The value of the label, again, depends on the multicluster mode:

`mirror.linkerd.io/exported: true`
> For gateway-based multicluster configurations. The service mirror will expect there to be a gateway for the remote cluster, and it will set up the mirrored Service to use it.

`mirror.linkerd.io/exported: remote-discovery`
> For Pod-to-Pod multicluster configurations. The service mirror will set up the mirrored Service to go directly to the original Pods.

It's also worth noting that the service mirror needs permission to talk to the remote cluster's Kubernetes API server. Credentials for this are handled by the Linkerd Link resource, created with the `linkerd multicluster link` CLI command.

Links and GitOps

Link resources are actually a little bit more imperative than they should be: running the `linkerd multicluster link` command creates a credentials Secret, a Link resource, and the service mirror controller. Unfortunately, it's extremely hard to replicate everything without actually running the command right now.

With all of that background, we can start setting up an example multicluster architecture.

Setting Up for Multicluster

Multicluster Linkerd *always* requires that you be able to route IP traffic between your clusters. In some cases, it also requires that all clusters have distinct, nonoverlapping cluster and service CIDR ranges.

Obviously, ensuring that these requirements are met is a bit outside the scope of the service mesh! However, to demonstrate a multicluster setup in this chapter, we'll be creating two k3d clusters, and we'll need to make sure the requirements are met when we do so. We'll call out where we're doing k3d-specific infrastructure things as we go.

First, as shown in Example 12-1, we'll create two k3d clusters attached to the same Docker network, and we'll give them independent cluster and service CIDRs so that we can use this setup either for gateway-based multicluster or for Pod-to-Pod multicluster mode.

This entire block is k3d-specific, unsurprisingly!

Example 12-1. Creating clusters

```
# Create cluster1
$ k3d cluster create cluster1 \
    --servers=1 \
    --network=mc-network \
    --k3s-arg '--disable=traefik@server:*' \
    --k3s-arg '--cluster-cidr=10.23.0.0/16@server:*' \
    --k3s-arg '--service-cidr=10.247.0.0/16@server:*' \
    --wait

# Create cluster2
$ k3d cluster create cluster2 \
    --servers=1 \
    --network=mc-network \
    --k3s-arg '--disable=traefik@server:*' \
    --k3s-arg '--cluster-cidr=10.22.0.0/16@server:*' \
    --k3s-arg '--service-cidr=10.246.0.0/16@server:*' \
    --wait
```

Note that both clusters are told to use the same Docker network (`--network=mc-network`), but they have independent, nonoverlapping CIDR ranges.

We'll continue by setting up IP routing between clusters, as shown in Example 12-2. The `docker exec` commands here are k3d-specific, but the idea of running the `ip route add` command on the Nodes themselves is actually not k3d-specific.

Example 12-2. Setting up IP routing

```
# For each cluster, we need its Node IP and Pod CIDR range.
$ cluster1_node_ip=$(kubectl --context k3d-cluster1 get node k3d-cluster1-server-0 \
  -o jsonpath='{.status.addresses[?(.type=="InternalIP")].address}')
$ cluster1_pod_cidr=$(kubectl --context k3d-cluster1 get node k3d-cluster1-server-0 \
  -o jsonpath='{.spec.podCIDR}')

$ cluster2_node_ip=$(kubectl --context k3d-cluster2 get node k3d-cluster2-server-0 \
  -o jsonpath='{.status.addresses[?(.type=="InternalIP")].address}')
$ cluster2_pod_cidr=$(kubectl --context k3d-cluster2 get node k3d-cluster2-server-0 \
  -o jsonpath='{.spec.podCIDR}')

# Once that's done, we'll run `ip route add` on each Node to set up IP
# routing. We only need to do this once per cluster because these are
# single-Node clusters.
$ docker exec -it k3d-cluster1-server-0 \
  ip route add ${cluster2_pod_cidr} via ${cluster2_node_ip}
$ docker exec -it k3d-cluster2-server-0 \
  ip route add ${cluster1_pod_cidr} via ${cluster1_node_ip}
```

Once we have routing set up, it's time to create new certificates using step, as shown in Example 12-3. As noted previously, you'll need to use the same trust anchor for every cluster, no matter what kind of cluster you're using.

Example 12-3. Creating certificates for multicluster

```
# First, create a trust anchor. This will be shared across all clusters.
$ step certificate create root.linkerd.cluster.local ca.crt ca.key \
  --profile root-ca --no-password --insecure

# Next, use the trust anchor to create identity issuer certificates
# (one for each cluster).
$ step certificate create identity.linkerd.cluster.local issuer1.crt issuer1.key \
  --profile intermediate-ca --not-after 8760h --no-password --insecure \
  --ca ca.crt --ca-key ca.key

$ step certificate create identity.linkerd.cluster.local issuer2.crt issuer2.key \
  --profile intermediate-ca --not-after 8760h --no-password --insecure \
  --ca ca.crt --ca-key ca.key
```

Finally, given our certificates, we can install Linkerd and the Viz extension! This is shown in Example 12-4.

Be Careful of Contexts!

We have personally made far more mistakes than we'd care to admit to when working with multicluster setups. A truly embarrassing amount of the time, the problem was because we ran a kubectl command against the wrong cluster—so pay attention to those --context arguments!

Alternatively, just set up a window for each cluster and work that way. This works well if you have separate Kubernetes configuration files and can set the KUBECONFIG variable differently depending on which cluster you want.

Example 12-4. Installing Linkerd

```
# Install Linkerd in cluster1...
$ linkerd install --context k3d-cluster1 --crds \
  | kubectl apply --context k3d-cluster1 -f -

$ linkerd install --context k3d-cluster1 \
  --identity-trust-anchors-file ca.crt \
  --identity-issuer-certificate-file issuer1.crt \
  --identity-issuer-key-file issuer1.key \
  | kubectl apply --context k3d-cluster1 -f -

$ linkerd viz install --context k3d-cluster1 |
  kubectl apply --context k3d-cluster1 -f -

$ linkerd check --context k3d-cluster1

# ...then repeat for cluster2.
$ linkerd install --context k3d-cluster2 --crds \
  | kubectl apply --context k3d-cluster2 -f -

$ linkerd install --context k3d-cluster2 \
  --identity-trust-anchors-file ca.crt \
  --identity-issuer-certificate-file issuer2.crt \
  --identity-issuer-key-file issuer2.key \
  | kubectl apply --context k3d-cluster2 -f -

$ linkerd viz install --context k3d-cluster2 |
  kubectl apply --context k3d-cluster2 -f -

$ linkerd check --context k3d-cluster2
```

At this point, we have to decide whether we're using a gateway-based or Pod-to-Pod multicluster architecture, because what we do from this point forward changes.

Continuing with a Gateway-Based Setup

If you want a Pod-to-Pod setup, skip ahead to "Continuing with a Pod-to-Pod Setup" on page 182.

To continue with gateway-based multicluster mode, we install the Linkerd Multicluster extension as shown in Example 12-5. This extension also ships with the core Linkerd CLI, so you needn't install an extra command to use it. This is the default way to install Linkerd Multicluster, since gateway-based multicluster mode predates Pod-to-Pod.

Example 12-5. Installing Linkerd Multicluster with gateways

```
$ linkerd multicluster install --context k3d-cluster1 |
  kubectl apply --context k3d-cluster1 -f -
$ linkerd multicluster check --context k3d-cluster1

$ linkerd multicluster install --context k3d-cluster2 |
  kubectl apply --context k3d-cluster2 -f -
$ linkerd multicluster check --context k3d-cluster2
```

After that, we'll need to link our clusters together using the gateways, as shown in Example 12-6.

k3d and --api-server-address

k3d clusters are weird: they always create Kubernetes contexts that say that the Kubernetes API server is on localhost. With our multicluster setup on the same Docker network, our cluster1 cannot use localhost to talk to cluster2, or vice versa.

Therefore, for k3d, we have to use --api-server-address to override the address with a routable IP address for the other cluster. This is specific to k3d.

Example 12-6. Linking the clusters with gateways

```
# Link cluster1 to cluster2. Again, --api-server-address is k3d-specific.
# PAY ATTENTION TO CONTEXTS! We run `linkerd multicluster link` in the
# cluster1 context, then apply it in the cluster2 context.
$ linkerd multicluster link --context k3d-cluster1 \
  --api-server-address https://${cluster1_node_ip}:6443 \
  --cluster-name k3d-cluster1 |
  kubectl apply --context k3d-cluster2 -f -
```

```
# Link cluster2 to cluster1. Again, --api-server-address is k3d-specific.
# PAY ATTENTION TO CONTEXTS! We run `linkerd multicluster link` in the
# cluster2 context, then apply it in the cluster1 context.
$ linkerd multicluster link --context k3d-cluster2 \
  --api-server-address https://${cluster2_node_ip}:6443 \
  --cluster-name k3d-cluster2 |
  kubectl apply --context k3d-cluster1 -f -

# Ensure everything is healthy (note that this will fail for k3d, even
# though things are working).
$ linkerd multicluster check

# Check on the gateways.
$ linkerd multicluster gateways --context k3d-cluster1
$ linkerd multicluster gateways --context k3d-cluster2
```

At this point, skip ahead to "Multicluster Gotchas" on page 183.

Continuing with a Pod-to-Pod Setup

If you want a gateway-based setup, go back to "Continuing with a Gateway-Based Setup" on page 181.

To continue with Pod-to-Pod multicluster mode, we install the Linkerd Multicluster extension as shown in Example 12-7, using the --gateway false flag.

Example 12-7. Installing Linkerd Multicluster Pod-to-Pod

```
$ linkerd multicluster install --gateway false --context k3d-cluster1 |
  kubectl apply --context k3d-cluster1 -f -
$ linkerd multicluster check --context k3d-cluster1

$ linkerd multicluster install  --gateway false --context k3d-cluster2 |
  kubectl apply --context k3d-cluster2 -f -
$ linkerd multicluster check --context k3d-cluster2
```

Now we need to link our clusters, as shown in Example 12-8. Again, we need the --gateway false flag (and we only need --api-server-address for k3d).

Example 12-8. Linking the clusters Pod-to-Pod

```
# Link cluster1 to cluster2. Again, --api-server-address is k3d-specific.
# PAY ATTENTION TO CONTEXTS! We run `linkerd multicluster link` in the
# cluster1 context, then apply it in the cluster2 context.
$ linkerd multicluster link --gateway false --context k3d-cluster1 \
  --api-server-address https://${cluster1_node_ip}:6443 \
  --cluster-name k3d-cluster1 |
  kubectl apply --context k3d-cluster2 -f -
```

```
# Link cluster2 to cluster1. Again, --api-server-address is k3d-specific.
# PAY ATTENTION TO CONTEXTS! We run `linkerd multicluster link` in the
# cluster2 context, then apply it in the cluster1 context.
$ linkerd multicluster link --gateway false --context k3d-cluster2 \
  --api-server-address https://${cluster2_node_ip}:6443 \
  --cluster-name k3d-cluster2 |
  kubectl apply --context k3d-cluster1 -f -

# Ensure everything is healthy (note that this will fail for k3d, even
# though things are working).
$ linkerd multicluster check
```

Multicluster Gotchas

Irrespective of whether you're setting up for gateway-based multicluster or Pod-to-Pod multicluster, there are two things that are always very important to bear in mind:

Directions, contexts, and links

Every linkerd multicluster link command creates a unidirectional link. Running a link command in the cluster1 context and applying it to the cluster2 context is giving cluster2 the permissions and DNS information needed to communicate with cluster1. Basically, running the link command in the cluster1 context gathers information and credentials *about* cluster1; applying it in the cluster2 context gives everything *to* cluster2.

In our example setup (whether gateway or Pod-to-Pod), we run two links, one in each direction. In most two-cluster setups, this makes sense, but it's definitely not required.

Checking Your connections

We've helped a lot of folks troubleshoot their multicluster setups, and the most common problem we've seen is a lack of connectivity between the clusters. When you're debugging multicluster setups, the first thing to check is *always* to make sure that you have the appropriate connectivity between your clusters.

You can usually do this very effectively simply by running a Pod in one cluster with tools like curl, dig, etc., and then trying to make simple HTTP calls to the other cluster.

Deploying and Connecting an Application

At this point, we have our clusters connected, and we need to begin taking advantage of our links. In Example 12-9 we will deploy the emojivoto sample application (*https://oreil.ly/qfGlx*) across two clusters.

Example 12-9. Deploying a multicluster application

```
# Pull down the luar repo if you don't already have it.
$ git clone https://github.com/linkerd-book/luar.git

# Create the emojivoto ns in each cluster.
$ kubectl apply --context k3d-cluster1 -f luar/multicluster/ns.yaml
$ kubectl apply --context k3d-cluster2 -f luar/multicluster/ns.yaml

# This will ensure that all new Pods come up with
# the Linkerd proxy.

# Start the backing services in cluster2.
$ kubectl apply --context k3d-cluster2 -f luar/multicluster/emoji.yaml
$ kubectl apply --context k3d-cluster2 -f luar/multicluster/voting.yaml

# Start the web frontend and traffic generator in
# cluster1.
$ kubectl apply --context k3d-cluster1 -f luar/multicluster/web.yaml

# Check on the Pods in each cluster.
$ kubectl get pods -n emojivoto --context k3d-cluster1
$ kubectl get pods -n emojivoto --context k3d-cluster2
```

At this point, the Pods will be running in each cluster, but they have no information about how to talk to each other. You can verify this simply by looking at the Services in each cluster, as shown in Example 12-10.

Example 12-10. Checking the Services in each cluster

```
$ kubectl get svc -n emojivoto --context k3d-cluster1
$ kubectl get svc -n emojivoto --context k3d-cluster2
```

To make emojivoto work in our scenario, we'll need to mirror services across the clusters. For each Service we want exported, we'll add the `mirror.linkerd.io/exported` label to it:

- If you're using gateway-based multicluster mode, use `mirror.linkerd.io/exported: true`, as shown in Example 12-11.

- If you're using Pod-to-Pod multicluster mode, use `mirror.linkerd.io/exported: remote-discovery`, as shown in Example 12-12.

Example 12-11. Exporting Services with gateways

```
$ kubectl --context=k3d-cluster1 label svc web-svc \
  -n emojivoto mirror.linkerd.io/exported=true
$ kubectl --context=k3d-cluster2 label svc emoji-svc \
  -n emojivoto mirror.linkerd.io/exported=true
$ kubectl --context=k3d-cluster2 label svc voting-svc \
  -n emojivoto mirror.linkerd.io/exported=true
```

Example 12-12. Exporting Services Pod-to-Pod

```
$ kubectl --context=k3d-cluster1 label svc web-svc \
  -n emojivoto mirror.linkerd.io/exported=remote-discovery
$ kubectl --context=k3d-cluster2 label svc emoji-svc \
  -n emojivoto mirror.linkerd.io/exported=remote-discovery
$ kubectl --context=k3d-cluster2 label svc voting-svc \
  -n emojivoto mirror.linkerd.io/exported=remote-discovery
```

In either case, if you check the Services in the emojivoto namespace, as shown in Example 12-13, you'll see the mirrored Services.

Example 12-13. Checking on mirrored Services

```
$ kubectl get svc -n emojivoto --context k3d-cluster1
$ kubectl get svc -n emojivoto --context k3d-cluster2
```

If using Pod-to-Pod multicluster mode, you can also use linkerd diagnostics endpoints to check that everything is working correctly, as shown in Example 12-14.

Example 12-14. Checking on Service endpoints

```
# Any valid Service DNS name should work here.
$ linkerd diagnostics endpoints --context k3d-cluster1 \
  emoji-svc-cluster2.linkerd-multicluster.svc.cluster.local
$ linkerd diagnostics endpoints --context k3d-cluster2 \
  web-svc-cluster1.linkerd-multicluster.svc.cluster.local
```

As implied by Example 12-14, mirrored Services appear as *serviceName-clusterName*; for example, the emoji-svc mirrored from cluster2 into cluster1 will appear as emoji-svc-cluster2.

This is a rare case where, by default, the application may have to change to work with Linkerd. The manifests that we applied in Example 12-9 have already been tweaked so that the emojivoto app uses the mirrored Service names, but you can also use an HTTPRoute and a placeholder Service to redirect traffic.

For example, suppose we want all traffic for emoji-svc to be redirected to emoji-svc-cluster2. We could start by creating a Service named emoji-svc with no selector, so that it's simply not possible for that Service to match any Pods. This is shown in Example 12-15.

Example 12-15. A placeholder emoji-svc Service

```
---
apiVersion: v1
kind: Service
metadata:
  name: emoji-svc
  namespace: emojivoto
spec:
  type: ClusterIP
  ports:
  - port: 80
    targetPort: http
```

We can then associate an HTTPRoute with the placeholder Service to redirect all the traffic, as shown in Example 12-16.

Example 12-16. Redirecting all traffic to the placeholder emoji-svc Service

```
---
apiVersion: policy.linkerd.io/v1beta3
kind: HTTPRoute
metadata:
  name: emoji-svc-route
  namespace: emojivoto
spec:
  parentRefs:
    - name: emoji-svc
      kind: Service
      group: ""
      port: 80
  rules:
  - backendRefs:
    - name: emoji-svc-cluster2
      port: 80
      weight: 100
    timeouts:
      request: 5s
```

Checking Traffic

At this point, traffic should be flowing across clusters and the emojivoto application should be working, as you should be able to see by pointing a web browser to the web-svc service in cluster1, as shown in Example 12-17.

Example 12-17. Checking out emojivoto with a browser

```
$ kubectl --context k3d-cluster1 port-forward -n emojivoto web-svc 8080:80 &

# Open a browser to http://localhost:8000/ here
```

You can also watch traffic flowing in the Linkerd Viz dashboard, accessible by running either command shown in Example 12-18, or by using the CLI commands in Example 12-19.

Example 12-18. Multicluster Linkerd Viz dashboard

```
$ linkerd  --context k3d-cluster1 viz dashboard
$ linkerd  --context k3d-cluster2 viz dashboard
```

Example 12-19. Multicluster Linkerd Viz CLI

```
$ linkerd viz stat service -n emojivoto --context k3d-cluster1
$ linkerd viz stat service -n emojivoto --context k3d-cluster2
```

However you look at it, you should be able to see traffic flowing across clusters.

Policy in Multicluster Environments

There's one more thing to cover before we close out the chapter. Linkerd policy is applicable not just within but also between clusters. However, as you saw in Figures 12-1 and 12-2, the two modes work differently. When using gateway-based multicluster mode, the gateway itself is where you need to apply any cross-cluster policy. It will accept policy configurations like any other workload in the mesh.

Pod-to-Pod multicluster mode has the advantage of preserving the identity of the originating workload when you make multicluster requests. That means you can set a policy directly on your target workload to only accept requests from the services that need to access it.

Summary

This chapter covered how multicluster architecture works in Linkerd and showed you how to set it up in a local environment. Linkerd's multicluster features are robust, powerful, and used at scale by some of the largest organizations in the world. Consider how a multicluster setup could impact your environment and if it's a good addition to your platform.

# CHAPTER 13

Linkerd CNI Versus Init Containers

In Chapter 2, we mentioned the init container a couple of times without ever talking about it in detail. The init container is one of the two mechanisms Linkerd provides for handling mesh networking in Kubernetes, with the other being the Linkerd CNI plugin. To understand what these do and why you'd choose one over the other, you need to understand what happens when a meshed Pod starts running.

As it happens, that's a much bigger, thornier issue than you might expect. We'll start by looking at vanilla Kubernetes, *without* Linkerd.

Kubernetes sans Linkerd

At its core, Kubernetes has a straightforward goal: manage user workloads so that developers can concentrate on Pods and Services without needing to worry too much about the underlying hardware. This is one of those things that's easy to describe, and fairly easy to use, but *extremely* complex to implement. Kubernetes relies on several different open source technologies to get it all done. Remember that we're talking about Kubernetes *without* Linkerd at this point—this is essentially your standard Kubernetes functionality.

Nodes, Pods, and More

The first area that Kubernetes has to manage is orchestrating the actual execution of workloads within a cluster. It relies extensively on OS-level isolation mechanisms for this task. Here are some key points to keep in mind:

- Clusters comprise one or more *Nodes*, which are physical or virtual machines running Kubernetes itself. We'll discuss Linux Nodes here.

- Since Nodes are entirely distinct from one another, everything on one Node is isolated from others.

- Pods consist of one or more *containers*, and they're isolated within the same Node using Linux `cgroups` (*https://oreil.ly/K1z3T*) and `namespaces`.

- Containers within the same Pod are allowed to communicate using *loopback* networking. Containers in different Pods need to use non-loopback addresses because Pods are isolated from each other. Pod-to-Pod communication is the same whether the Pods are on the same Node or not.

- An important point is that Linux itself operates at the Node level: Pods and containers don't have to run separate instances of the OS. This is the reason that isolation between them is so critical.

This layered approach, shown in Figure 13-1, lets Kubernetes orchestrate the distribution of workloads within the cluster, while keeping an eye on resource availability and usage: workload containers map to Pods, Pods are scheduled onto Nodes, and all Nodes connect to a single flat network.

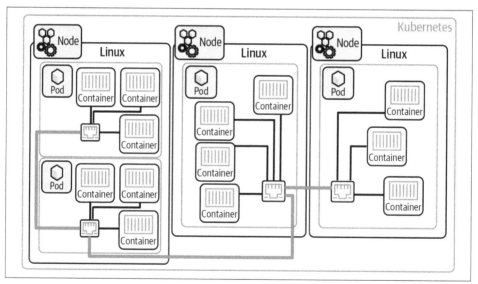

Figure 13-1. Clusters, Nodes, Pods, and containers

(What about Deployments, ReplicaSets, DaemonSets, and such? They're all about hinting to Kubernetes where the Pods they create should be scheduled; the actual scheduling mechanism underneath is the same.)

Networking in Kubernetes

The other major area that Kubernetes manages is the network, starting with the fundamental tenet that every Pod must see a flat and transparent network. Every Pod should be able to communicate with all others, on any Node. This means that every Pod must have its own IP address (the *Pod IP*).

Containers or Pods?

The requirement is actually that *any two containers* must be able to talk to each other, but IP addresses are allocated at the Pod level—multiple containers within one Pod share the same IP address.

While it's possible to have a workload use Pod IPs directly to communicate with other workloads, it's not a good idea due to the dynamic nature of Pod IPs: they change as Pods cycle. It's a better idea to use Kubernetes Services in most cases.

Services are rather complex, as we discussed briefly in Chapter 5:

- Creating a Service triggers the allocation of a DNS entry, so workloads can refer to the Service by name.
- Creating a Service also triggers allocation of a unique IP address for the Service, distinct from any other IP address in the cluster. We call this the Service IP.
- The Service includes a *selector*, which defines which Pods will be associated with the Service.
- Lastly, the Service gathers the Pod IP addresses of all its matching Pods and maintains them as its endpoints.

This is all shown in Figure 13-2—which, sadly, is still a *simplified* view of Services.

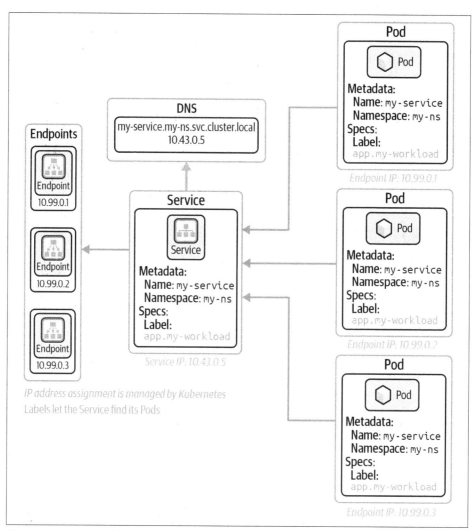

Figure 13-2. Kubernetes Services and addressing

When a workload attempts to connect to a Service, Kubernetes will, by default, select one of the Service's endpoints and route the connection there. This allows Kubernetes to perform basic load balancing of connections, as shown in Figure 13-3:

- Connections within Pods happen over localhost so that they stay within the Pod.

- Connections to other workloads hosted on the same Node stay internal to the Node.

- Connections to workloads hosted on other Nodes are the only ones that transit the network.

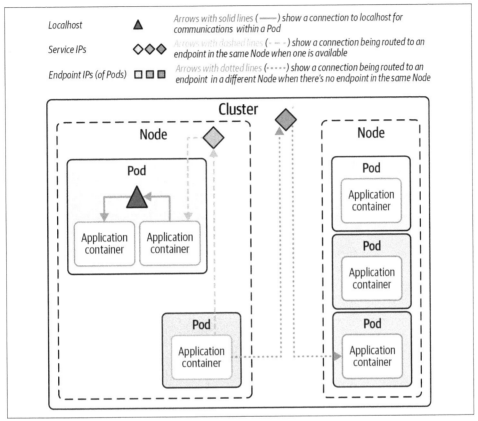

Figure 13-3. Kubernetes basic network routing

To make this all work, Kubernetes relies on the networking mechanisms built into the core of the Linux kernel.

The Role of the Packet Filter

The Linux kernel has long included a powerful *packet filter* mechanism to inspect network packets and make decisions about what to do with each one. Possible actions the packet filter system can take include letting the packet continue as is, modifying the packet, rerouting the packet, or even discarding it entirely.

Kubernetes takes extensive advantage of the packet filter to handle the complexities of routing traffic among an ever-changing set of Pods within a cluster. For instance, the filter can intercept a packet sent to a Service and rewrite it to go to a specific Pod IP instead. It can also distinguish between a Pod IP on the same Node as the sender and one on a different Node, and manage routing appropriately. If we zoom in a bit on Figure 13-3, we get the more detailed view in Figure 13-4.

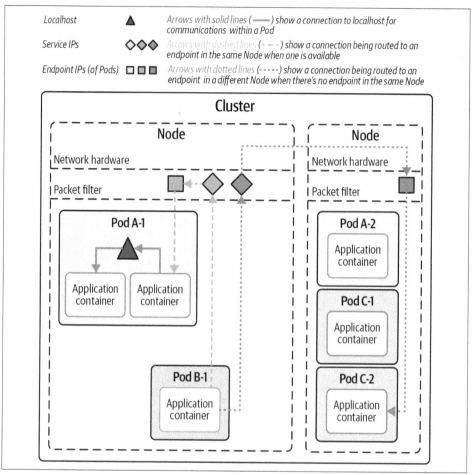

Figure 13-4. Kubernetes and the packet filter

Let's follow the dotted-line connection shown in Figure 13-4, from Pod B-1 all the way to Pod C-2:

- The application container in Pod B-1 makes a connection to the Service IP address for Service C.

- The packet filter sees a connection from a local container to the Service IP, so it redirects that connection to the Pod IP of either Pod C-1 or Pod C-2. By default, the choice is random for each new connection (though the exact configuration of the cluster's networking layer can change this).

- In this case, the Pod IP is on a different Node, so the network hardware gets involved to communicate over the network to the second Node.

- On the second Node, the packet filter sees the connection coming over the network to a Pod IP address, so it hands the connection directly to the Pod, choosing a container based on the port number.

For the dashed-line connection shown between Pod B-1 and Pod A-1, the process is the same, except that the network hardware has no role to play since the connection is entirely contained within one Node. In all cases, the containers see a simple, flat network, with all containers living in the same IP address range—which, of course, requires Kubernetes to continuously update the packet filter rules as Pods are created and removed.

Alphabet Soup: iptables, nftables, and eBPF

There have been several implementations of the packet filter over time, and you may hear people use the name of a specific implementation when talking about this topic. The most common as of this writing is `iptables`, but a newer `nftables` implementation is becoming more popular.

You might also find this whole bit reminding you of the filtering technology known as eBPF, which makes a lot of sense since eBPF is particularly good at this kind of packet wizardry. However, many implementations predate eBPF and don't rely on it.

The Container Networking Interface

Since networking configuration is a rather low-level aspect of Kubernetes, the details tend to depend on which Kubernetes implementation is in use. The Container Network Interface (CNI) is a standard designed to offer a consistent interface for managing dynamic network configurations; for example, the CNI provides mechanisms for allocating and releasing IP addresses within specific ranges, which Kubernetes uses in turn to manage the IP addresses associated with Services and Pods.

The CNI doesn't directly provide mechanisms for managing packet filtering functionality, but it does allow for *CNI plugins*. Service meshes—including Linkerd—can use these plugins to implement the packet filtering configuration they need to function.

> **CNI Versus CNI**
>
> There are many implementations of the CNI, and a given Kubernetes solution often allows a choice between several different CNI implementations (for example, k3d uses Flannel (*https://oreil.ly/ GIVvg*) by default as its networking layer, but it can be easily switched to Calico (*https://oreil.ly/YSSts*)).

The Kubernetes Pod Startup Process

When all is said and done, here's what Kubernetes needs to do to start a Pod:

1. Locate a Node to host the new Pod.

2. Run any CNI plugins defined by the Node within the new Pod's context. The process fails if any plugin doesn't work.

3. Execute any init containers defined for the new Pod, in the order they're defined. Again, the startup process fails if any don't work.

4. Launch all the containers defined by the Pod.

During the initiation of the Pod's containers, it's important to note that the containers will start in the order outlined by the Pod's spec. However, Kubernetes will *not* wait for one container to start before moving on to the next, unless a container has a postStartHook defined. In that case, Kubernetes will start that container, run the postStartHook to completion, and only then proceed to start the next container. We'll talk more about this in "Container ordering" on page 199.

Kubernetes and Linkerd

Any service mesh introduces complexities into startup, and Linkerd is no exception. The first concern is that Linkerd has to inject its proxy into application Pods, and the proxy has to intercept network traffic going into and out of the Pod. Injection is managed using a mutating admission controller. Interception is more complex, and Linkerd has two ways to manage it: you can use either an init container or a CNI plugin.

The Init Container Approach

The most straightforward way for Linkerd to configure networking is via an init container, as shown in Figure 13-5. Kubernetes ensures all init containers are run to completion, in the order they're mentioned in the Pod's spec, before any other containers start. This makes the init container an ideal way to configure the packet filter.

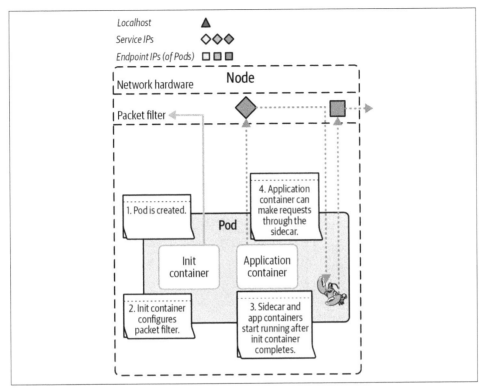

Figure 13-5. Startup with the init container

The downside here is that the init container requires the NET_ADMIN capability to perform the required configuration. In many Kubernetes runtimes, this capability simply isn't available, and you'll need to resort to the Linkerd CNI plugin.

Also, the OS used in some Kubernetes clusters may not support the older iptables binary used by default in Linkerd (this typically comes into play with the Red Hat family). In these instances, you'll need to set proxyInit.iptablesMode=nft to instruct Linkerd to use iptables-nft instead. (This isn't the default setting because iptables-nft isn't universally supported yet.)

The Linkerd CNI Plugin Method

In contrast, the Linkerd CNI plugin simply requires that you install the plugin prior to installing Linkerd itself. It doesn't need any special capabilities, and the CNI plugin will operate every time a Pod starts, configuring the packet filter as required, as shown in Figure 13-6.

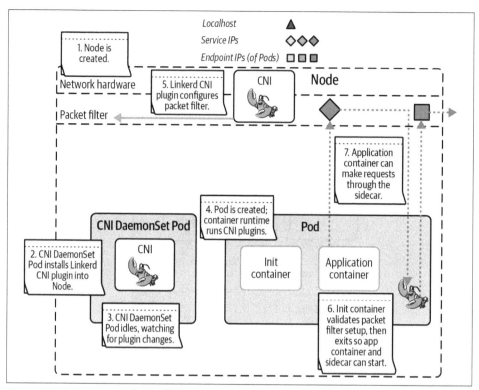

Figure 13-6. Startup with the CNI plugin

The main complication here is that the CNI was originally designed for the people setting up the cluster in the first place, rather than people using it after it's been created. As a result, the CNI assumes that the ordering of CNI plugins is handled completely outside the Kubernetes environment. This has turned out to be less than ideal, so most CNI plugins these days (including the Linkerd CNI plugin) are written to try to do the right thing no matter what the cluster operators did.

In the case of the Linkerd CNI plugin, when it's enabled Linkerd installs a DaemonSet designed to arrange for the Linkerd CNI plugin to always run last. This allows other plugins the chance to configure what they need before Linkerd jumps in to enable the Linkerd proxy to intercept traffic.

When using the CNI plugin, Linkerd will still inject an init container. If you're using a version of Linkerd prior to `stable-2.13.0`, this will be a no-op init container that, as the name suggests, essentially doesn't do much. From `stable-2.13.0` onward, the init container will verify that the packet filter is correctly configured. If it's not, the container will fail, prompting Kubernetes to restart the Pod. This helps to avoid a startup race condition (more on this in the next section).

Races and Ordering

As you can see, the startup process in Kubernetes can be complex—which means that there are several different ways things can fail.

Container ordering

As mentioned previously, containers are launched in the order they appear in the Pod's spec, but Kubernetes doesn't wait for a given container to start before launching the next one (except for init containers). This can cause trouble during Linkerd's startup: what if the application container begins running and tries to use the network before the Linkerd proxy container is functioning?

Starting with Linkerd 2.12, there's a postStartHook on the Linkerd proxy container to deal with this. When a container has a postStartHook, Kubernetes starts the container, then runs the postStartHook to completion before starting the next container. This gives containers a straightforward way to ensure ordering.

The Linkerd proxy's postStartHook won't complete until the proxy is actually running, which forces Kubernetes to wait until the proxy is functional before starting the application container. If necessary, this functionality can be disabled by setting the annotation config.linkerd.io/proxy-await=disabled. However, we recommend leaving it enabled unless there's a compelling reason to do otherwise!

CNI plugin ordering

There are several ways CNI plugin ordering can cause confusion:

DaemonSets versus other Pods
> Kubernetes treats DaemonSet Pods just like any other Pods, which means that an application Pod might be scheduled before the Linkerd CNI DaemonSet can install the Linkerd CNI plugin! This implies that the Linkerd CNI plugin won't run for the application Pod, which in turn means that the application container(s) won't have a functioning Linkerd proxy.
>
> Before Linkerd stable-2.13.0, there was no way to catch this, and the application container would simply never be present in the mesh. As of stable-2.13.0, though, the init container checks that the packet filter has been configured correctly. If it's not, the init container will exit, causing a crash loop from Kubernetes's point of view, which will make the failure obvious.

Multiple CNI plugins
> In most cases, a given Kubernetes installation will use more than one CNI plugin. While the Linkerd CNI DaemonSet puts a lot of effort into allowing the Linkerd CNI plugin to run last, and to not disrupting other CNI plugins, it's not perfect. If this goes wrong, the Pod will (again) probably never appear to be in the mesh.

Misconfigured CNI

It's always possible to simply misconfigure the Linkerd CNI plugin when you install it in the first place. For example, when running k3d, it's necessary to supply the plugin with certain paths, and if these are wrong, the plugin itself won't work. This might cause application Pods to silently fail to launch, or it might cause "corrupt message" errors to show up in the proxy logs:

```
{ "message": "Failed to connect", "error": "received corrupt message" }
```

The only real saving grace of CNI issues is that they're typically pretty obvious, conspicuous errors: you'll see linkerd check fail, or Pods won't start, or similar things. On the other hand, *resolving* the failures can be tricky and depends greatly on the specific CNI involved, so in general we recommend sticking with the init container mechanism where possible.

Summary

There's a lot of complexity to the Kubernetes startup process—especially with Linkerd—but there are also some simple recommendations to help keep everything going smoothly:

- Keep Linkerd up-to-date! Recent versions have added some really helpful things for startup.

- Use proxy-await unless you have a *very* good reason to disable it. It'll make sure that your application code has a working mesh before starting.

- Stick with the init container if you can. If not, just use the CNI plugin, but if your cluster can run with the init container, it's probably simplest to do so.

# CHAPTER 14

Production-Ready Linkerd

Once you've deployed Linkerd, your next task is to appropriately harden your environment for production usage. As you prepare, it's valuable to familiarize yourself with the resources available to you. Linkerd users have access to two basic sets of resources:

- Community-provided resources, which are free to use and a great source of information for everyone
- Commercial resources from Buoyant, the creators of Linkerd

For the purposes of this book we're going to avoid going into the paid resources. If you'd like more information on Buoyant's commercial offerings, visit the Buoyant website (*https://buoyant.io*).

Linkerd Community Resources

The Linkerd community is active on GitHub (*https://oreil.ly/n6j1e*), Slack (*https://slack.linkerd.io*), and the CNCF mailing list (*https://oreil.ly/w5dIi*). Beyond that, there are a number of useful guides and resources online.

If you're looking to learn more about running Linkerd in production, the Buoyant production runbook (*https://oreil.ly/kCfO5*) is actively updated as Linkerd versions change and contains lots of important information.

Getting Help

Community support for Linkerd is mostly provided by volunteer community members in the Linkerd Slack or directly by the maintainer and contributor community on GitHub. It's important that users trying to get help from the open source community understand that you have a responsibility to carefully test all changes you make to Linkerd. When seeking help for Linkerd, you should be sure to clearly articulate the problem you're facing and, if possible, provide clear steps to reproduce the issue. The hardest task for maintainers or volunteer community members will always be understanding and testing any particular problems that come up.

Responsible Disclosure

If you run into a security issue with Linkerd, the project maintainers kindly ask that you send a private email to *cncf-linkerd-maintainers@lists.cncf.io*. The maintainers will acknowledge your report and provide you additional information as they investigate the disclosure. You can subscribe to Linkerd vulnerability notifications at the cncf-linkerd-announce mailing list (*https://oreil.ly/HIc0c*).

Kubernetes Compatibility

Linkerd is tested with all currently active Kubernetes versions. Each version's release notes contain the minimum supported Kubernetes version.

Going to Production with Linkerd

With that out of the way, we can dive into going to production with Linkerd.

Stable or Edge?

For production use, your simplest path is going to be running a release from the stable channel, such as Buoyant Enterprise for Linkerd. Running an edge-channel release in production is definitely possible, though.

If you decide to run edge releases in production, it is *critical* that you carefully read the release notes for any release you're considering and that you give feedback about your experience to the Linkerd maintainers. The simplest way to do this is via the community Slack (*https://slack.linkerd.io*). Discussions or issues on GitHub (*https://oreil.ly/y0Zut*) are also a great way to reach the Linkerd team.

Preparing Your Environment

The first step in making sure that your environment is ready for Linkerd is always to run the CLI's preflight check:

```
$ linkerd check --pre
```

This will verify that your environment is ready to run Linkerd, paying particular attention to Kubernetes permissions.

Beyond the preflight check, you also need to make sure that you understand your environment's particular security requirements. For example:

- If you can't allow your Pods NET_ADMIN permissions, you'll need to use the Linkerd CNI plugin.
- If you're using the Kubernetes tainting mechanism and you have applied custom taints to the Nodes where you'll be running the Linkerd control plane, you'll need to add tolerations to the Linkerd deployments.
- If you use network policies to segregate traffic, you'll need to make sure that your policies allow communication between the Linkerd control plane and its proxies. You may also want to consider using the Linkerd policy mechanisms for application-aware policy enforcement.

In addition to communications, you'll also need to consider how you'll handle adding your application to the mesh, as discussed in Chapter 4. For example, will you use namespace injection or workload injection? These aren't likely to be terribly complex decisions, but it's still a good idea to think about them ahead of time.

To recap, you add a workload to the mesh by instructing the Linkerd proxy injector, a mutating webhook, to add a proxy to a Pod at Pod creation time. That instruction can be passed by adding an annotation at either the namespace, workload, or Pod level:

```
linkerd.io/inject: enabled
```

For production use, we recommend that you add the annotation at the namespace or workload level. This will generally be the simplest way to manage meshing application workloads, since it doesn't require altering individual Pod manifests. (There are some situations in which you may need to add the proxy directly to a Pod, as discussed in Chapter 6, but they're few and far between.)

In either case, you'll want to configure your deployment tooling to add the appropriate annotations during the deployment process, to ensure that your workloads are all appropriately meshed. This is also the time to add any exceptions to the cluster-wide configuration for skip and opaque ports, as discussed in Chapter 4.

Explicitly Enabling Injection

Remember that if you are adding the Linkerd proxy-injection annotations at the namespace level, you can still override the injection behavior on individual workloads by adding the following annotation to a Deployment:

```
linkerd.io/inject: disabled
```

Configuring Linkerd for High Availability

If you're deploying Linkerd in production, it means you've decided to add critical security, observability, and reliability features to your production application. Good for you! Unfortunately, all that new functionality comes with some very real costs. Linkerd is now in the critical operating path for your most critical workloads. If Linkerd suffers a catastrophic failure, you're likely to suffer a very real application outage, or at the very least a degradation in service.

In order to mitigate these risks, the Linkerd project defines and supports *high availability* (HA) mode. HA mode modifies the way Linkerd is deployed, as shown in Figure 14-1.

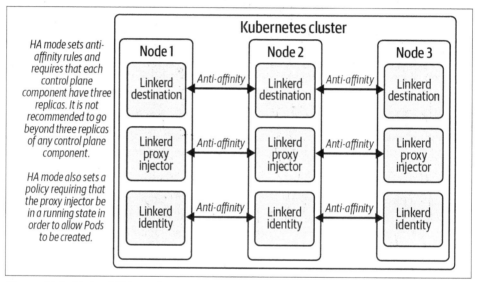

Figure 14-1. Linkerd HA mode

Always Run HA in Production

We *strongly* recommend HA mode for any production use of Linkerd. If you don't explicitly install in HA mode, your Linkerd installation will have several single points of failure that could cause downtime for your application.

What does HA mode do?

High availability mode makes a few significant changes to your Linkerd control plane install. You can find all the details about exactly what HA mode changes in the latest documentation (*https://oreil.ly/eDjOq*), and we strongly encourage you to review this documentation when upgrading to make sure that you're working with the latest information.

The basic configuration, though, has been fairly consistent over time. In broad strokes, HA mode:

Runs three replicas

In HA mode, each control plane component runs three replicas rather than just one, to prevent failure of a single replica from taking down the whole mesh.

Sets anti-affinity

Additionally, HA mode creates anti-affinity rules that prevent any single Node from running more than one replica of any control plane component. This prevents a single Node failure from taking down the entire mesh.

Tightens resource limits

HA mode establishes much more aggressive CPU and memory resource requests and limits than non-HA mode, to prevent any runaway processes from causing more widespread problems for the cluster as a whole.

 Verifying Requests and Limits

These more aggressive limits set by HA mode function well for many organizations, but you should view them as just a starting point: they may not be what your organization needs. It's important to actively monitor the Linkerd control plane's actual resource usage for your installation and tune the requests and limits as needed.

In particular, a control plane component that hits its memory limit will be OOMKilled and then restarted. This can be easy to miss if it happens infrequently, but if it happens consistently, you will likely suffer a production incident.

Makes the `proxy-injector` *mandatory*

In HA mode, the `proxy-injector` component of the Linkerd control plane is *required* to be healthy before *any* Pod is allowed to be scheduled. This reflects the fact that Linkerd is commonly responsible for ensuring secure communications within your application. It is likely to be better to fail to start an application Pod than to allow it to run without having Linkerd's proxy present to make it part of the mesh.

It's important to realize, though, that this requirement is enforced using a cluster-wide admission webhook, and as such it affects *every* Pod in the cluster, not just application workloads. This means that you *must* exempt critical cluster infra-structure namespaces, such as `kube-system`, from having the policy enforced.

To exempt a namespace, apply the following label to the namespace:

```
config.linkerd.io/admission-webhooks: disabled
```

> **No Admission Webhook for Infrastructure!**
>
> You *must* exempt infrastructure namespaces from the HA admission webhook. If you don't, you can easily end up deadlocked, with Linkerd waiting for system infrastructure while system infrastructure is waiting for Linkerd.

High availability installation with Helm

We recommend using Helm for production Linkerd installs, including high availability installs. A complicating factor is that high availability installations are much more likely than other installations to need customized values for Helm. To make this a bit easier, the Linkerd Helm chart includes a values file that you can use as a basis for your high availability installation.

We recommend that you always refer to the latest high availability installation instructions (*https://oreil.ly/GLiFw*) when deploying Linkerd HA with Helm. A brief overview of the process at the time of writing is shown in Example 14-1.

Example 14-1. Installing Linkerd in HA mode with Helm

```
# Add the Linkerd stable repo
$ helm repo add linkerd https://helm.linkerd.io/stable

# Update your Helm repositories
$ helm repo update

# Pull down the latest version of the chart
$ helm fetch --untar linkerd/linkerd-control-plane

# Examine linkerd-control-plane/values-ha.yaml and edit if needed. The
# edited file should be placed in version control and, as new charts are
# released, periodically compared with the new values-ha.yaml files.

# Install the Linkerd CRDs
$ helm install linkerd-crds linkerd/linkerd-crds \
  -n linkerd --create-namespace

# Install the Linkerd control plane
# Note the added reference to the values-ha.yaml file
$ helm install linkerd-control-plane \
  -n linkerd \
  --set-file identityTrustAnchorsPEM=ca.crt \
  --set-file identity.issuer.tls.crtPEM=issuer.crt \
  --set-file identity.issuer.tls.keyPEM=issuer.key \
  -f linkerd-control-plane/values-ha.yaml \
  linkerd/linkerd-control-plane

# Ensure your install was successful
$ linkerd check
```

As noted in the comments, you should keep your version of *values-ha.yaml* in version control. It's an important resource for reinstallations and disaster recovery.

High availability installation with the CLI

While we don't generally recommend CLI-based installs for production environments, you can use the Linkerd CLI to output deployment YAML configured with all the HA options and then use this YAML as the basis for your actual install process.

To do this, use the `linkerd install` command with the `--ha` flag, and save the resulting YAML to a file:

```
$ linkerd install --ha > linkerd-ha.yaml
```

You can then put *linkerd-ha.yaml* in version control and edit it as needed.

Monitoring Linkerd

There are commercial providers that will automatically configure Linkerd monitoring and alerting. For those of you looking to monitor Linkerd yourselves, we recommend you establish monitors to ensure Linkerd remains highly available in your environment.

Certificate Health and Expiration

The most common cause of Linkerd outages is expired certificates. Both the trust anchor and identity issuer certificates must be valid at all times to avoid downtime. As such, carefully monitoring your certificates to be certain that you always renew them before they expire is crucial.

The `linkerd check` command will begin warning you when your root or issuer certs will expire in less than 60 days.

> **Never Let Your Certificates Expire**
>
> Because Linkerd requires mTLS connections between Pods by default, the health and security of the certificates it uses are absolutely critical to the healthy operation of the mesh—and thus your platform. If certificates expire, or can't be generated for new Pods, *you will incur downtime.*
>
> This is the most common cause of downtime in production Linkerd clusters. Understanding and monitoring your Linkerd certificates is vital.

Control Plane

Linkerd's control plane is vital to the normal operation of your platform. You should collect and measure Linkerd proxy metrics for the control plane, like success rates, latency, and requests per second. Alert on aberrant behavior and investigate situations where the success rates drop below 100%.

You should also closely monitor the resource consumption of the control plane and ensure it never gets close to its CPU or memory limits.

Data Plane

The Linkerd proxy tends to be fairly uncomplicated and straightforward to operate. That being said, it's important to ensure the proxies aren't consuming more resources than they should be: if they are, it can indicate excessive traffic or other issues. Monitor the resource usage on your proxies, and ensure that their resource requests and limits match what they need in order to handle application traffic.

It's also wise to ensure you are monitoring the versions of the Linkerd proxies in your environment. The proxy will be deployed with the version defined by the proxy injector at the time a Pod is created. If your Pods aren't restarted on a regular basis, the proxy version can get out of sync with the control plane. You will want to ensure your proxies are always within at least one major version of the control plane.

Metrics Collection

Any production installation of Linkerd also needs to account for what you will do with the metrics data generated by Linkerd. Linkerd proxies are constantly collecting useful information about the traffic going into and out of their Pods, and all this information is made available in such a way that any tool compatible with Open-Telemetry should be able to access it. (Linkerd has also long provided open source configuration details for configuring Prometheus to scrape metrics from Linkerd.)

Linkerd is not itself a monitoring tool (though Linkerd Viz can consume metrics and display many useful things about them); instead, it is designed to provide metrics to whatever monitoring solution is already in use in your environment. Whatever that is, one of the most important long-term tasks facing a platform engineer responsible for a production Linkerd installation is creating a plan for collecting, storing, and using all the metrics generated by Linkerd, since effective long-term monitoring is extremely valuable for understanding the behavior and health of your apps.

Linkerd Viz for Production Use

The Linkerd Viz extension consumes metrics provided by Linkerd, using them to enable some powerful diagnostics for Linkerd and providing a basic open source dashboard (shown in Figure 14-2) to make some of these metrics more easily visible. As of Linkerd 2.12, the core visibility data available from the CLI—from metrics to the state of a multicluster gateway—requires the Linkerd Viz extension to be installed.

LINKERD	Namespaces						
CLUSTER	HTTP Metrics						≡
Namespaces	Namespace ↑	Meshed	Success Rate	RPS	P50 Latency	P95 Latency	P99 Latency
Control Plane	default	0/0	---	---	---	---	---
DEFAULT ▼	emojivoto	4/4	92.14% ●	6.15	1 ms	4 ms	8 ms
WORKLOADS	kube-node-lease	0/0	---	---	---	---	---
Cron Jobs	kube-public	0/0	---	---	---	---	---
Daemon Sets	kube-system	0/5	---	---	---	---	---
Deployments	linkerd	3/3	100.00% ●	2.4	1 ms	4 ms	5 ms
Services	linkerd-jaeger	3/3	100.00% ●	1.3	1 ms	1 ms	2 ms
Jobs	linkerd-viz	5/5	100.00% ●	3.23	2 ms	71 ms	94 ms
Pods							
Replica Sets							
Replication Controllers							

Figure 14-2. The Linkerd Viz dashboard

Though Linkerd Viz is not *required* for production use, we generally recommend installing it. Running Viz in production requires careful attention to three areas:

Prometheus and Linkerd Viz
When you install Linkerd Viz, it can install a Prometheus instance for you. *This Prometheus instance is not recommended for production use*, since it uses an in-memory data store for metrics. As it saves more metrics data, it will fill up its available memory and crash, losing all the metrics data it had saved up to that point. In a busy production system, this can happen multiple times a day.

To use Linkerd Viz in production, therefore, you'll need to use a different Prometheus instance with persistent storage. The full procedure for externalizing Prometheus is shown in Example 10-9. You can also review the official docs on externalizing Prometheus (*https://oreil.ly/i5knP*).

Always Use Your Own Prometheus

We'll say it one more time: *do not use the Prometheus installed by Linkerd Viz in production*. It stores your metrics only in RAM, and you *will* lose any historical data when it restarts.

Chapter 10 has more details on the right way to deal with metrics.

Securing the Linkerd Viz dashboard

The open source Linkerd Viz dashboard provides access to important information about your cluster, including metrics, Linkerd Tap, and more. For ease of experimentation, it does not include any authentication mechanism; as such, we *do not recommend* this configuration for production.

If you intend to make the Linkerd Viz dashboard available in production, we *strongly recommend* limiting access to it using your ingress controller as well as Linkerd authorization policy. You can learn more about ingress controllers in Chapter 5, and more about exactly how to secure the Linkerd Viz dashboard in the Linkerd docs (*https://oreil.ly/Ivenb*).

Securing Linkerd Tap

Linkerd Tap allows operators to view the metadata about requests between applications in your environment. Though it cannot ever access unencrypted message bodies, it is still important to secure access to Linkerd Tap since many organizations include potentially sensitive information in their URLs or headers that should not be exposed to everyone with access to the cluster. Access to Linkerd Tap is provided via the `linkerd-linkerd-tap-admin` ClusterRole.

You can read more about securing Tap traffic in the Linkerd docs (*https://oreil.ly/wjWnb*), but the most basic operation here is to give a Kubernetes account permission to access Linkerd Tap. That can be done with the role binding shown in Example 14-2.

Example 14-2. Accessing Linkerd Tap

```
$ export USER=<target_username>
$ kubectl create clusterrolebinding \
  "${USER}"-tap-admin \
  --clusterrole=linkerd-linkerd-viz-tap-admin \
  --user="${USER}"
```

Accessing Linkerd Logs

The Linkerd control plane and the Linkerd proxies all emit log information, accessible using `kubectl logs`, that can be valuable for troubleshooting any active incidents or investigating anomalous behavior. Each log message emitted has an associated *log level*:

ERROR

Messages that indicate serious problems with Linkerd that must be resolved in order to continue operating the mesh

WARNING

Messages that indicate problems that should be resolved but won't prevent the mesh from functioning

INFO

Informational messages

DEBUG

Messages that are only for debugging and usually require knowledge of Linkerd to interpret

By default, Linkerd components are configured to emit messages at the INFO level and higher. If necessary, you can override this configuration so that Linkerd will emit DEBUG messages too. (It is not recommended to turn off INFO-level messages.) Switching the log level requires a restart for the control plane, though Linkerd proxies can change their log level at runtime.

You should only switch Linkerd to emit DEBUG-level log messages while actively troubleshooting an issue; emitting DEBUG-level logs has real performance implications for Linkerd itself, and the extra log volume can quickly overwhelm log aggregators.

On that note, when monitoring your Linkerd environment it's worthwhile to monitor the log level of your Linkerd components to ensure they haven't been mistakenly left emitting DEBUG logs.

Upgrading Linkerd

Linkerd is designed to be safe to operate and upgrade. Upgrades within the same major version are generally safe and, if high availability mode is configured, can be confidently performed without any loss of functionality. That being said, in all cases it's wise to test your upgrades, and upgrade processes, in your nonproduction environments before moving to production.

When using releases from the stable channel, remember that major version upgrades, unlike minor version upgrades, can contain breaking changes. Linkerd 2.10, 2.11, and 2.12 all contained significant changes to the operation of Linkerd that required many users to change their deployment strategies or carefully test the behavior of their applications. It is incumbent on you as the platform operator to carefully read the release notes for a new major version before deploying and test your upgrade process before moving to production.

Never Skip Major Versions

When upgrading, *never* skip major versions; for example, an upgrade from 2.12.5 to 2.14.3 is *not supported*. Upgrades are tested only across a single major version; attempting to skip will land you in uncharted territory and could easily cause downtime.

Note that you should *always* read the upgrade instructions for a given release before upgrading; for example, Linkerd 2.12 added a new step to the process. This is especially important when using releases from the edge channel! You can find the latest instructions in the Linkerd upgrade documentation (*https://oreil.ly/Mmou7*).

As with Linkerd installs, the project supports two main pathways for upgrading.

Upgrading via Helm

Using Helm is the recommended method for production installations and upgrades.

Read the Instructions

Remember to read the Linkerd upgrade instructions (*https://oreil.ly/7IhPt*) before starting the upgrade!

Here's the process:

1. Ensure that the control plane itself is healthy and that Linkerd is running cleanly:

   ```
   $ linkerd check
   ```

2. If `linkerd check` reveals any issues, address them *before* moving forward. Trying to upgrade when the control plane is not functioning correctly can cause major problems.

3. Once you know that the control plane is running smoothly, pull down updates to your Helm repositories:

   ```
   $ helm repo update
   ```

4. Next, update the Linkerd Helm charts. Note that as of Linkerd 2.12, there are two distinct Helm charts, and you need to run upgrades for both.

   First, upgrade the Linkerd CRDs:

   ```
   $ helm upgrade linkerd-crds -n linkerd linkerd/linkerd-crds
   ```

   Once that's done, upgrade the control plane itself:

   ```
   $ helm upgrade linkerd-control-plane \
       -n linkerd linkerd/linkerd-control-plane
   ```

5. Once again, ensure that the control plane is healthy:

```
$ linkerd check
```

Upgrading via the CLI

Linkerd's CLI has an `upgrade` command that will output YAML that can be directly applied to your Kubernetes cluster to upgrade the Linkerd control plane. While we generally recommend using Helm to upgrade Linkerd, the Linkerd CLI may better fit some workflows.

Read the Instructions

Remember to read the Linkerd upgrade instructions (*https:// oreil.ly/7IhPt*) before starting the upgrade!

The basic process for upgrading the via the CLI is:

1. Ensure that the control plane itself is healthy and that Linkerd is running cleanly:

   ```
   $ linkerd check
   ```

2. If `linkerd check` reveals any issues, address them *before* moving forward. Trying to upgrade when the control plane is not functioning correctly can cause major problems.

3. Start the upgrade process itself by installing the latest version of the Linkerd CLI. This allows the CLI to fetch the latest versions of the various Linkerd installation resources:

   ```
   $ curl --proto '=https' --tlsv1.2 -sSfL https://run.linkerd.io/install | sh
   ```

   Confirm you're running the latest version with:

   ```
   $ linkerd version --client
   ```

4. Upgrade the control plane running in the cluster:

   ```
   $ linkerd upgrade \
       | kubectl apply --prune -l linkerd.io/control-plane-ns=linkerd -f -
   ```

   Using the `--prune` flag ensures that resources that are no longer required are removed from your cluster.

5. Once again, ensure that the control plane is healthy:

```
$ linkerd check
```

Readiness Checklist

There's a lot separating a small demo environment from a major production environment, as we've just covered! The following checklist covers some of the most important things to consider when taking Linkerd into production:

- I've run Linkerd's preflight checks with my installation credentials.
- I'm mirroring the Linkerd images into my own internal registry.
- I'm confident I have the capacity on my cluster to run Linkerd's control plane in high availability mode.
- I have a plan to run Linkerd in HA mode.
- I have created my own certificates for Linkerd.
  - I have a plan to securely store and rotate those certificates.
  - I have created monitors to ensure I will be notified before my certificates expire.
- I have identified the various non-HTTP workloads in use in my environment.
  - I am aware of which ones are in the mesh and which are not.
- I have annotated the `kube-system` namespace to ensure it will operate normally without the proxy injector being available.
- I have ensured the `linkerd` namespace will not be configured for auto-injection.
- I have ensured the `kube-system` namespace will not be configured for auto-injection.
- I am aware of any other namespaces that I need to ensure do not get injected by the proxy.
  - I have exempted them from the injector failure policy.
- I have a plan for adding the appropriate annotations to my workloads.

- I have a plan for gathering and storing Linkerd metrics.
- I have tooling in place to ensure Linkerd is healthy and that I will be notified if there is an issue.

If you are able to check off most or all of these items, you are well on your way to being able to confidently run Linkerd in production.

Summary

In this chapter, we covered many of the core tasks and concerns involved with running Linkerd in production. No two organizations have identical operational constraints and requirements, so, as with everything else in technology, you should be prepared to adapt this advice to your real-world circumstances. If you have particular operational concerns, or want help running Linkerd, we recommend connecting with the Linkerd community or establishing a commercial relationship with a vendor that provides support or management for Linkerd.

# CHAPTER 15

Debugging Linkerd

If you've come this far, you understand how valuable a tool Linkerd can be for a platform to provide. It secures your apps, provides powerful insights into those applications, and can account for underlying application and network issues by making your connections more reliable. In this chapter, we're going to look at what to do when you need to troubleshoot Linkerd itself.

In all cases, the first step when diagnosing an issue with Linkerd is to use the Linkerd CLI's built-in health checking tool by running linkerd check, as we discussed in more detail in Chapter 6. linkerd check is a very quick way to pinpoint many of the most common issues with Linkerd installations; for example, it can immediately diagnose expired certificates, which is the most common issue that causes Linkerd outages in practice.

Diagnosing Data Plane Issues

Linkerd is somewhat famous for not requiring a ton of hands-on work with the data plane; however, it's still useful to be able to do some basic troubleshooting. Many proxy issues end up involving fairly similar sets of solutions.

"Common" Linkerd Data Plane Failures

While Linkerd is generally a fault-tolerant service mesh, there are a few conditions that we see arise more than others. Knowing how to tackle these can be extremely helpful.

Pods failing to start

If you run into a situation where injected Pods are failing to start, the first step will be to identify exactly where the failure is occurring. This is where the `kubectl describe pod` and `kubectl logs` commands can provide a lot of useful information.

It's often most useful to start by describing a failing Pod, to get a sense of what Kubernetes believes has happened. For example, did the Linkerd init container fail? Did the Pod get killed because its probes never reported ready? This information can help you decide which containers to pull logs from, if you need the logs.

If the failing containers belong to the application rather than to Linkerd, you'll likely be best off looking at non-Linkerd-specific potential causes, like a failing common dependency, or perhaps Nodes running out of resources. If it's Linkerd containers failing, though, the second step is to understand whether the failure is affecting all new Pods or only some new Pods:

Single Pod failure

   If a single Pod is failing, you'll want to look at the characteristics of that Pod. Which containers are failing to start? Is it the proxy, an init container, or the application itself? If other Pods are starting normally, it isn't a systemic issue and you'll need to dive into the particulars of the specific Pod.

All Pods are failing to start

   If the failure is happening on all new Pods, you likely have a more serious systemic issue. As noted before, the most common reason that all Pods fail to start is a certificate issue. The `linkerd check` command will reveal this kind of issue immediately, which is why we recommend running it first.

   Another possible—though uncommon—issue is that the Linkerd proxy injector isn't running or is unhealthy. Note that when running Linkerd in HA mode, which (as discussed in Chapter 14) we recommend for production use, Kubernetes will refuse to start any new application Pods until the injector is healthy.

A subset of Pods is failing to start

   If only some new Pods are failing to start, it's time to begin isolating what common factors exist across those Pods:

   - Look at the output of `kubectl get pods -o wide` to see if they've been scheduled on the same Node or Nodes.

   - Look at the `kubectl describe pod` output: are the init containers failing to complete successfully?

   - If you're using the Linkerd CNI plugin, you'll want to check the state of the network validator, and you may need to restart the CNI container for that Node.

- If you're not using the Linkerd CNI plugin, take a look at the output of `kubectl logs` for the Linkerd init container. If it failed to complete successfully, try to see what is unique about the Node it's running on.

Intermittent proxy errors

Intermittent proxy errors can be one of the hardest issues to solve. Any intermittent problem with the proxy is necessarily difficult to catch and address. When running Linkerd in production, it's important to build in monitoring to catch errors including:

Permission denied events
> These represent either a dangerous misconfiguration in your platform or a genuine threat to your environment. You'll need to collect and analyze the logs from the Linkerd proxies in order to detect these events.

Protocol detection timeouts
> Protocol detection, discussed in Chapter 4, is the process of Linkerd automatically identifying traffic between two Pods. It's an important step that occurs before the proxy can begin sending and receiving traffic. On occasion, protocol detection can time out and then fall back to treating a connection as a standard TCP connection. That means the proxy will introduce an unnecessary 10-second delay, and then the connection will not benefit from Linkerd's ability to do things like request-level routing.
>
> Protocol detection timeout events usually indicate a port that should be marked as skipped or opaque (again, this is discussed in Chapter 4). In particular, the proxy will never be able to correctly perform protocol detection for server-speaks-first protocols. If you're using Linkerd's policy resources, you have the ability to declare the protocol on a given port. This allows you to skip protocol detection entirely and will improve the overall availability, as well as security, of your applications.
>
> A proxy may also be unable to handle protocol detection if it is overloaded.

Out of memory events
> An out of memory event for the proxy represents a resource allocation issue. It's important to monitor, test, and manage the resource limits for the Linkerd proxy. It intercepts and manages the traffic going into and out of your applications, and managing its resources is a core responsibility of the platform team.
>
> Ensure you're providing the proxy with the resources it needs to handle the traffic flowing through it, or you're going to have a bad day.

HTTP errors
> In general, Linkerd will reuse persistent TCP connections between your Pods and will surface any application-level errors that occur, so if your applications have

any kind of underlying configuration issues, you should see the errors that your application is actually generating.

However, there are times that the Linkerd proxy will itself respond to a request with an immediate 502, 503, or 504, and it's important to understand what can cause these:

502s

It's not uncommon for new service mesh users to see an uptick in the occurrence of 502 errors when they begin adding applications to the service mesh. This is because whenever Linkerd sees a connection error between proxies, it will show up as a 502. If you're seeing a large number of 502 errors in your environment, consult the Linkerd docs (*https://oreil.ly/77p8P*) for more troubleshooting steps you can take.

503s and 504s

503s and 504s show up when a Linkerd proxy finds that requests are overwhelming a workload's ability to respond.

Internally, a Linkerd proxy maintains a queue of requests to dispatch. In normal operation, an incoming request spends almost no time in the queue: it is queued, and the proxy chooses an available endpoint for the request and then immediately dispatches it.

However, suppose there's a massive flood of incoming requests, far too many for the workload to handle. When the queue gets too long, Linkerd begins *load shedding*, where any new request that arrives gets an immediate 503 directly from the proxy. To stop load shedding, the incoming request rate needs to slow enough for the requests in the queue to get dispatched, allowing the queue to shrink.

Also, the pool of endpoints is dynamic: a given endpoint can be removed from the pool by circuit breaking, for example. If the pool ever becomes completely empty—i.e., there are *no* available endpoints—then the queue enters a state called *failfast*. In failfast, all requests in the queue immediately get a 504 response, and then Linkerd shifts to load shedding, so new requests again get a 503.

To get out of failfast, some backend has to become available again. If you got into failfast due to circuit breaking marking all your backends unavailable, the most likely way you'll get out is that circuit breaking will allow a probe request to go through, it'll succeed, and then the backend will be marked available again. At that point Linkerd can bring the workload out of failfast and things will start being handled normally again.

503 Is Not the Same as 504!

Note the different responses there! 504s happen *only* at the point where the load balancer enters failfast, while 503s indicate load shedding—which could be due to failfast, or could be due to too much traffic.

Setting Proxy Log Levels

In normal operation, the Linkerd proxy does not log debugging information. If needed, you can change the Linkerd proxy's log level without needing to restart the proxy.

Debug Logging Can Be Expensive

If you set too verbose a log level, the proxy will consume dramatically more resources, and its performance will degrade. Do not modify the proxy's log level unless you need to, and be sure to reset the log level when you're not actively debugging.

When you need to start debugging, you can turn on debug-level logging as shown in Example 15-1.

Example 15-1. Turning on debug logging

```
# Be sure to replace $POD_NAME with the name of the Pod in question.
$ kubectl port-forward $POD_NAME linkerd-admin

$ curl -v --data 'linkerd=debug' -X PUT localhost:4191/proxy-log-level
```

Once you've finished debugging, be sure to turn *off* debug-level logging, as shown in Example 15-2. *Don't leave the proxy running debug-level logging for longer than you need to*: it *will* impact performance.

Example 15-2. Turning off debug logging

```
# Be sure to replace $POD_NAME with the name of the Pod in question.
$ kubectl port-forward $POD_NAME linkerd-admin

$ curl -v --data 'warn,linkerd2_proxy=info' -X PUT localhost:4191/proxy-log-level
```

Log levels were discussed in "Accessing Linkerd Logs" on page 210; you can find more information about configuring the Linkerd proxy's log level in the official Linkerd docs (*https://oreil.ly/GNv9I*).

Debugging the Linkerd Control Plane

Linkerd's control plane is broken down into the core control plane and its extensions (such as Linkerd Viz and Linkerd Multicluster). Since every component of the control plane uses a Linkerd proxy to communicate, you can take advantage of Linkerd's observability for debugging.

Linkerd Control Plane and Availability

The control plane is a part of all mesh operations, so its health is critical. As we mentioned at the start of this chapter, the fastest way to get a good overview of the health of the control plane—outside of paying for a managed service—is to run `linkerd check`.

`linkerd check` will go through a series of detailed tests and will validate that there are no known misconfigurations. If there are issues, `linkerd check` will point you to documentation about how to fix the problem.

Always Start with linkerd check

It's hard to overstate how useful `linkerd check` is. Whenever you see anything that looks unusual about your mesh, *always* start with `linkerd check`.

It's also good to realize that `linkerd check` is deliberate about the order in which it runs its tests: it starts by running all the tests for the core control plane, then moves on to each extension in sequence. Within each section, `linkerd check` generally performs its tests in sequence, with each one needing to pass before the next is able to run. If a test fails, the section it's in and its position within the section can itself give you a lot of information about where to start debugging.

The Core Control Plane

The core control plane controls Pod creation, certificate management, and traffic routing between Pods. As discussed in Chapter 2, the core control plane consists of three main components: the proxy injector, the destination controller, and the identity controller. We'll dive into failure modes for those components now and what to do about them.

Use HA Mode in Production

Any instance of Linkerd that is running in production must use high availability mode—no exceptions! Without HA mode, a single failure in the control plane can put the whole mesh at risk, which is not acceptable in production. You can read more about HA mode in Chapter 14.

The identity controller

Any failure in the identity controller will impact the issuing and renewing of workload certificates. If a Pod can't get a certificate at start time, the proxy will fail to start and it will log a message to that effect. On the other side, if a proxy's certificate expires, it will begin emitting log messages that it failed to renew and will be unable to connect to any new Pods.

As of this writing we're familiar with only two known failure modes for the identity controller:

Expired certificates
> When you install Linkerd, you provide the control plane with a trust anchor certificate and an identity issuer certificate, as discussed at length in Chapter 7. If the identity issuer certificate expires, the identity controller will no longer be able to issue new certificates, which will cause a mesh-wide outage as individual proxies become unable to establish secure connections with one another.

Never Let Your Certificates Expire

Expired certificates will cause your entire mesh to grind to a halt, and they are *the* most common cause of production Linkerd outages. You *must* regularly monitor the health of your certificates.

Identity controller overload
> Linkerd's identity controller is accessed every time a new meshed Pod is created. As such, it's possible—though difficult—to overwhelm the identity controller by creating a very large number of Pods. This will manifest as long delays in Pod creation and a large number of messages about certificate creation in the identity controller's logs.

> The simplest way to deal with an overloaded identity controller is horizontal scaling: add more replicas to the `linkerd-identity` deployment in the `linkerd` namespace. You might also want to consider allowing it to request more CPU.

The destination controller

Linkerd's destination controller is responsible for providing the individual proxies with their routing information as well as providing details about the effective policy for your environment. It is critical to the normal operations of the mesh, and any degradation should be considered a critical issue to be addressed immediately. There are two main areas to be aware of here:

Memory

> The destination controller's memory usage scales linearly with the number of endpoints in your cluster. For most clusters, this results in the destination controller consuming a fairly consistent amount of memory over time. In turn, this means that if the destination controller gets OOMKilled by Kubernetes, it is very likely to reach its memory limit and get OOMKilled again every time it restarts. Therefore, it's important to actively monitor and manage the memory limits on the destination controller.

Proxy cache

> The Linkerd proxy maintains a cache of endpoints that can be reused by the proxy in the event that the destination controller is unavailable. By default, the proxy will cache its endpoint list for 5 seconds and maintain that cache as long as it gets reused in any given 5-second interval. You can configure that timeout with the `outboundDiscoveryCacheUnusedTimeout` property of the `linkerd-control-plane` Helm chart. Increasing the timeout will increase your overall resiliency in the face of a destination controller outage, particularly for services that see less traffic.

The proxy injector

Linkerd's proxy injector is a mutating webhook that acts in response to Pod creation events. Of all the elements in the core control plane, the proxy injector is the one least likely to see issues, but it's important to actively monitor its health:

- In HA mode, if the proxy injector crashes, new Pods will not be allowed to start until the proxy injector is back online.

- In non-HA mode, if the proxy injector crashes, new Pods won't be injected into the mesh until it's back online.

Use HA Mode in Production

It should be clear from the above description why it's so important to use high availability mode in production. You can read more about HA mode in Chapter 14.

Linkerd Extensions

No Linkerd extensions are in the critical path to mesh operations, but many users of Linkerd use the Linkerd Viz extension, in particular, to gather additional details about the operation of their services. In the event that you're seeing aberrant behavior from Linkerd Viz, `linkerd check` will almost always show you what the failure is, and generally the best remediation is to upgrade or reinstall the extension.

The one exception to this "turn it off and on again" approach to troubleshooting Linkerd Viz is if you're using its built-in Prometheus instance. As we discussed in Chapter 14 and elsewhere, the built-in Prometheus instance stores metrics only in memory. This means that as you add more metrics data, it *will* periodically get OOMKilled by Kubernetes, and you will lose whatever data it had stored. This is a known limitation of the built-in Prometheus.

Do Not Use the Built-in Prometheus in Production

It should be clear from the previous description that you *must not use the built-in Prometheus instance in production*. You can read more about this in Chapter 14.

Summary

In general, Linkerd is a well-behaved, fault-tolerant mesh—especially in HA mode. However, as with all software, things can go wrong. After reading this chapter, you should have an idea of where to start looking when they do.

Index

TLS, 18, 81
authorization
    explicit authorization of Linkerd policy, 97
    microservice overreach as security issue, 5
    principle of least privilege, 5
AuthorizationPolicy resources, 100, 102

B

booksapp application
    installing booksapp, 124
    observability
        about, 141-142
        cloning booksapp repository, 142
        gathering application metrics, 143
        ServiceProfiles built with booksapp, 147
        setting up your cluster, 142
    route-based policy, 122
        configuring booksapp policy, 125
        HTTPRoute and health checks, 127, 129
        infrastructure policy, 125
        multiple identities in same MeshTLSAu-
            thentication, 136
        multiple workloads in a single Server
            definition, 134
        read-only access, 127-135
        reenabling the traffic generator, 138-139
        write access enabled, 135-137
budgeted retries, 155
    configuring the budget, 159
    counted retries versus, 155
    default retry budget, 158
bug reports via linkerd check command, 68
Buoyant, Inc.
    founding of, 13
    Helm for Linkerd in production, 31, 94, 206
        upgrading Linkerd, 212
    Linkerd as first service mesh, 1, 13
    Linkerd history, 13-15
    Linkerd production runbook, 201

C

Calico CNI, 196
call graph, 7
cert-manager (Venafi), 88, 89
    automatic certificate management via, 89
        configuring for Linkerd, 91-94
        installing cert-manager, 90
        installing Linkerd using cert-manager,
            94

external agent documentation URL, 91
certificates
    automatic management via cert-manager,
        89
        configuring for Linkerd, 91-94
        installing cert-manager, 90
        installing Linkerd using cert-manager,
            94
    deployment of Linkerd
        planning, 25, 27
        specifying in CLI install, 30
        specifying in Helm install, 31, 33
    ingress controllers, 51
    Linkerd and, 83
        certificate management, 84, 89
        certificates that are required, 27
        identity issuer certificate, 85
        never let certificates expire, 84, 88, 207,
            223
        trust anchor certificate, 84, 85
        workload certificates, 27, 83, 84, 86
    linkerd identity command for Pods, 72
    mTLS, 82
        Linkerd and mTLS, 83
        service mesh mTLS, 81
    multicluster setups, 176
        creating certificates, 179
    TLS, 18, 81
        Linkerd deployment planning, 25, 27
        service mesh mTLS, 81
    trust hierarchy, 82
certifying authorities (CAs), 18
    multicluster setups, 176
CIDR (Classless Inter-Domain Routing), 46
    documentation URL, 46
    multicluster setups
        CIDR ranges distinct, 178
        setting up, 178
    NetworkAuthentication CIDR ranges, 131
circuit breaking, 170
    annotations, 170
    documentation URL, 170
    enabling, 170
    not all failures hidden, 172
    service overload avoided, 6
    tuning, 171
Classless Inter-Domain Routing (see CIDR)
cleartext used within cluster, 55

same for multiple containers in one Pod, 191
   communication via Kubernetes Services, 191
   Service IP address load balanced, 57
IP routing between clusters, 178
   setting up, 178

J

Jaeger instance with Linkerd Jaeger extension, 23
   not for production, 23

K

k3d clusters in multicluster setup, 178-180
   Calico CNI available, 196
   Flannel CNI used by k3d, 196
   localhost context override, 181
k3s cluster for Linkerd deployment, 29
   k3d tool, 29
      provisioning a Kubernetes cluster, 29
keypairs of public and private keys, 18
   certifying authorities, 18
   identity issuer certificate, 86
   Linkerd trust anchor, 85
   mTLS certificates, 82
   rotating the keys, 18, 82
      Linkerd install from CLI, 30
      rotating the certificates, 87
kube-system namespace never injected into mesh, 41
KUBECONFIG in multicluster setups, 180
kubectl
   Linkerd deployment, 29
      testing connection to new cluster, 29
   Linkerd logs, 210
Kubernetes
   first release (2015), 13
   k3d clusters in multicluster setup, 178-180
      Calico CNI available, 196
      Flannel CNI used by k3d, 196
      localhost context override, 181
   k3s cluster for Linkerd deployment, 29
      k3d tool, 29
      provisioning a Kubernetes cluster, 29
   Linkerd and, 196
      init container approach, 196
      Linkerd CNI plugin approach, 197
   Linkerd exclusive support for, 15

operational simplicity, 15
   workloads, Pods, and services, 26
multiple processes versus multiple machines, 3
Pod startup process, 196
   CNI plugin ordering, 199
   container ordering, 199
   Pods failing to start, 199, 218
resource limits, 47
sidecar containers, 16
   admission controller, 19, 38-41
   resource limits, 47
without Linkerd, 189
   Kubernetes CNI, 195
   networking, 191-193
   orchestrating workload execution, 189
   packet filter role, 193-195
Kubernetes API
   inbound policy changes, 105
   Kubernetes resources
      linkerd inject command, 70
      resource limits, 47
   Linkerd management via, 15
Kubernetes CNI (Container Network Interface), 195
Kubernetes ingress controller, 60

L

l5d-dst-override header, 58, 59
   injected to every request, 59
latency, 8
   as sidecar issue, 10
Linkerd
   about, 1
      open source, 13
   architecture, 15
      certifying authorities, 18
      control plane, 19
      extensions, 20
      Kubernetes exclusive support, 15
      Kubernetes sidecar admission controller, 19, 38-41
      Kubernetes sidecar containers, 16
      Linkerd CNI plugin, 23
      Linkerd Jaeger extension, 22
      Linkerd Multicluster extension, 22
      Linkerd Service Mesh Interface extension, 23
      Linkerd Viz extension, 20-22

multicluster application deployment, 184
Services versus, 37
workloads versus, 37
Services
definition, 37
three distinct parts, 56, 191
ingress mode, 58
parentRefs versus backendRefs, 166
Pod communication via Kubernetes Services, 191
Pod IP addresses as endpoints of Service, 56, 153, 192
service mirror, 176
credentials via Linkerd Link, 177
multicluster application deployment, 184
services versus, 37
sidecar model, 10
adding workloads to the mesh, 38
annotation values, 40, 47
configuring protocol detection, 45
injecting all workloads in namespace, 40
injecting individual workloads, 40
Kubernetes admission controller, 19, 38
Kubernetes resource limits, 47
opaque versus skip ports, 44
protocol detection, 42-46
proxy injector configuration options, 42
when not to, 41
debug sidecar via linkerd inject, 71
Kubernetes sidecar containers, 16
Linkerd architecture, 16
skip ports, 44
configuration, 35, 45
documentation URL, 35
ingress controller incoming ports, 54
Smallstep CLI to generate certificates, 31
step as deployment tool, 29
stable release channel, 26
step CLI deployment tool, 29
generating certificates, 31
success rate of requests, 8

T

tampering as security issue, 4
Tap component of Linkerd Viz extension, 21
installing, 144
observability in Linkerd, 143
data stored in Prometheus, 146
ServiceProfile built with Tap, 146

securing, 210
documentation URL, 210
Tap injector, 21
TLS status validation, 144
timeouts, 159
configuring, 160-162
documentation URL, 161
HTTP 504 returned, 159
protocol detection timeouts, 219
TLS (Transport Layer Security), 17
about, 80-82
RFC 8446 URL, 80
ingress controllers, 51
Tap validating status, 144
X.509 certificates, 18, 81
Linkerd deployment planning, 25, 27
mTLS and Linkerd, 83
service mesh mTLS, 81
traffic, 8
multicluster setups, 187
traffic generator reenabled, 138-139
traffic shifting, 162
Gateway API HTTPRoute resource, 162, 169, 185
header-based routing (A/B testing), 162, 168
HTTPRoute with placeholder Service, 185
service mirror, 176, 184
setting up podinfo, 163-165
weight-based routing (canary), 162, 165-168
Transport Layer Security (see TLS)
troubleshooting (see debugging)
trust anchor certificate, 27, 84, 85
Linkerd install from CLI, 30
Linkerd install via Helm, 31, 33
rotating the certificates, 87
documentation URL, 88
rotating whole cluster, 89
same trust anchor to multiple clusters, 85, 176
setting up, 179
trust hierarchy of certificates, 82
multicluster setups, 85, 176

U

upgrading Linkerd, 211
CLI for upgrading, 213
documentation URL, 212
Helm for upgrading, 212
major version upgrades, 211

About the Authors

Jason Morgan is a DevOps practitioner who has helped many organizations on their cloud native journeys. Jason helps teams adopt cloud native ways of working so they can deliver for their customers and learn how to go fast forever. Jason has given talks, written a number of articles, and contributes to the CNCF.

Flynn is a technical evangelist at Buoyant working on spreading the good word about Linkerd, Kubernetes, and cloud native development in general. He is also the original author and a maintainer of the Emissary-ingress API gateway, also a CNCF project. His career in computing spans more than 40 years and runs the gamut from bringup on bare metal to distributed applications, with a common thread of communications and security throughout.

Colophon

The animal on the cover of *Linkerd: Up and Running* is the European lobster, or common lobster (*Homarus gammarus*).

This bluish crustacean is found in the eastern Atlantic Ocean, from as far north as Norway to Morocco; throughout much of the Mediterranean Sea; and along the eastern coast of the Black Sea. Though their ranges don't overlap, the European lobster is closely related to the American lobster.

Like their American relatives, European lobsters are opportunistic feeders, combing the seabed at night for invertebrates such as crabs, starfish, sea urchins, and even other lobsters. They use their larger crusher claw to break open any shells or carapaces and their smaller ripper claw to tear their food up. Interestingly, the "teeth" (or tooth-like structures) of the lobsters are actually in their stomachs!

Lobster has played an important role in human culinary history for thousands of years. In fact, a partial claw of the common lobster was found among kitchen detritus excavated from a seventh-century BCE village near Sardinia, and *Apicius* (a fifth-century CE Roman cookbook) includes a recipe for lobster croquettes. Yet lobster has not always been a luxury food fetching a premium price. When the first European settlers reached North America, lobsters were so plentiful that they purportedly washed ashore "in piles of two feet high." Due to their abundance, lobsters were cheap to acquire and thus gained a reputation as food for the poor.

The European lobster today remains relatively abundant, with a stable population and broad geographic range. As such, they have been classified by the IUCN as a species of least concern from a conservation standpoint. Many of the animals on O'Reilly covers are endangered; all of them are important to the world.

The cover illustration is by Karen Montgomery, based on an antique line engraving from Dover's *Animals*. The series design is by Edie Freedman, Ellie Volckhausen, and Karen Montgomery. The cover fonts are Gilroy Semibold and Guardian Sans. The text font is Adobe Minion Pro; the heading font is Adobe Myriad Condensed; and the code font is Dalton Maag's Ubuntu Mono.

O'REILLY®

Learn from experts.
Become one yourself.

Books | Live online courses
Instant answers | Virtual events
Videos | Interactive learning

Get started at oreilly.com.

Printed in the USA
CPSIA information can be obtained
at www.ICGtesting.com
JSHW050021170424
61274JS00005B/33